Wild Game Cookery

Third Edition, Revised and Expanded

Down-Home Recipes for Foods from the Wild

J. Carol Vance

The Countryman Press
Woodstock, Vermont

Library of Congress Cataloging-in-Publication Data
Vance, J. Carol, 1938-
    Wild game cookery : down-home recipes for foods from the wild / J. Carol
Vance. — 3rd ed., rev. and expanded.
        p.   cm.
    Includes index.
    ISBN 0-88150-419-X (alk. paper)
    1. Cookery (Game) I. Title.
TX751.V36 1998
641.6'91—dc21   98-3279
                                                                          CIP

Text and cover design by Faith Hague
Cover art: "After the Hunt (1884)" by William Meredith Harnett,
    courtesy of The Butler Institute of American Art, Youngstown, Ohio
Published by The Countryman Press
PO Box 748, Woodstock, Vermont 05091

Distributed by W. W. Norton & Company, Inc.
500 Fifth Avenue, New York, NY 10110

Printed in Canada

10 9 8 7 6 5 4

Dedication

This book is dedicated to the memory of my mother, Jenet, who knew all along that I was coming back to Benton to live, whose spirit willed me here, and who understood that I needed to be surrounded by the village that raised me.

It is also dedicated to the people who believed in me, supported me, and loved me, always—my brother and his family, my children, Scott and Karen, their families, and my wonderful grandsons, Austin and Ethan, who are the lights of my existence.

Contents

Preface

How my life has changed since I began writing my first cookbook in 1980! At that time my children, Scott and Karen, were in college, I was earning my last degree in education, and approaching my twentieth year in the classroom. Since then, I have learned to navigate life alone, traveled to almost every corner of the world, and celebrated the weddings of both my children. Now, I have the companionship of many old friends, the excitement of new friends, and the great joy of grandchildren, who live very close and share my life.

I grew up eating sausage, scrapple, ring bologna, home-cured hams, and bacon; these foods were a great influence and probably sparked my interest in food and my love for cooking. Back then we ate "jarred" fruits and vegetables, and cottage cheese with apple butter on top. Mother made yellow tomato jam, and we slathered her homemade strawberry jam on top of crisply fried scrapple from the store. Summers filled the Benton Meat Market with fruit and vegetables from local fields, and my all-time favorite was raspberries with heavy cream for breakfast.

Wild Game Cookery and *Fish and Fowl Cookery* have gone through several editions since then, although my writing career was put on hold by a two-and-a-half-year adventure in Guatemala. In addition to exploring Central America with other adventurers, I supervised beginning teachers and then became the principal of a private, bilingual school in Guatemala City. During those years I developed a penchant for gingerroot, chilies, black beans, plantains, mangoes, papayas, carambolas, cilantro, and salsa, salsa, salsa . . . Those experiences certainly influenced my cooking, particularly my use of herbs and spices.

Now I find myself back in the little town where I grew up, living in my childhood home, writing, cooking, gardening, and sewing. With the perspective of an adult, I now realize that my special childhood village is still a cohesive and supportive community where we all take care of each other. Benton beats with the rhythm of cooperation and caring. Whether it's sharing rides into the city, making hospital visits, or preparing food for shut-ins, this is a town of which I'm proud to be a part.

And now, in addition to writing, my family and I are involved in a cottage industry. Instead of sides of beef hanging in the old butcher shop, Santas of all sizes line the walls and watch over us as my sister-in-law Ruth Vance and I sew, and niece Misho Vance sculpts, to create our Images of Christmas Santas that are selling from coast to coast. So here I go again on a new adventure. May life be ever full of them.

Introduction

In researching this new combined and expanded edition of my two previous books, *Wild Game Cookery* and *Fish and Fowl Cookery*, the first thing I did was update the sources for obtaining wild game commercially. Since I first wrote *Wild Game Cookery*, the American palate has become more sophisticated, with venison and wild boar from Australia and Scotland as well as commercially raised rabbit, pheasant, and quail now finding their way to tables in the finest restaurants from New York to Seattle. And that was just the beginning. Now there are many domestic sources for commercially raised game and organic food.

During that research, I discovered that one of America's original organic farms was practically in my backyard. Since 1946, Walnut Acres, in Penns Creek, Pennsylvania, has been devoted to raising certified organic products, including fruits, vegetables, poultry, and beef. Because my books are devoted to the original organic meat, I was gratified to find that the popularity of organic meat and game has grown tremendously since I researched the first book.

You don't have to be a hunter to cook wild game. Game meats for discerning and gourmet palates are now as close as the telephone or the internet. Information for ordering is included in the *Sources* section of this book. And therein seems to lie the main difference between food purists and sportspersons—the source. Some hunt and forage. Others raise or buy their food. But whatever the source, this book addresses game preparations that range from simple recipes to gourmet dinners.

As I confessed in the introduction to the first edition of *Wild Game Cookery*, many of my recipes were adapted from those that originally called for domestic meats such as beef, chicken, and pork. And indeed, the recipes in this new volume can all be adapted for use with domestic meats and farmed or ranched game as well.

My original motivation in writing a cookbook was to get the wild game from the field to the table. Many sportspeople still take to the woods in the time-honored tradition, but often the cook in the kitchen just doesn't know what to do when presented with a saddle of venison. My first book, *Wild Game Cookery,* was written to take the mystery out of wild game preparation. In it I showed home cooks how to make nutritious meals quickly and easily using whatever game their hunters brought to the table. For instance, Indian Venison, with only two ingredients, was designed to get that game out of the freezer and onto the table. In other words, I feel that harvesting game should not be any different from going to a store and paying good money for meat or fowl. If you pay for it, you bring it home and prepare it. Likewise, if you take an animal, you should be committed to using it. First and foremost, that is what this book is all about.

In the years since I first put pen to paper, not only wild game but natural and organic foods as well have grown in popularity. Consumers are looking for pure and healthy food. They are eating less fat and watching calories like never before. In reworking both books and revising many recipes, I paid new attention to fat and cholesterol content. Many recipes

COMPARATIVE FAT CONTENT OF DOMESTIC MEAT AND WILD GAME

Meat, 3 oz, cooked	Fat (g)	Calories	Cholesterol (mg)
Antelope	2.67	150	126
Beef (select eye of round)	3.50	155	69
Beef (select tenderloin)	10.32	211	83
Caribou	4.42	167	109
Chicken (dark meat, no skin)	9.73	205	93
Chicken (light meat, no skin)	4.51	173	85
Duck	11.20	201	69
Elk	1.90	146	73
Lamb (choice loin chops)	9.76	202	87
Moose	0.97	134	78
Pork (loin chop)	7.21	194	78
Rabbit	6.31	154	64
Salmon	5.00	140	60
Turkey (dark meat, no skin)	7.22	187	85
Turkey (light meat, no skin)	3.22	157	69
Veal	6.94	175	106
Venison	3.19	158	112

here have been revised to reflect a more health-conscious eating style, and some high-fat preparations have been eliminated. However, the remaining high-fat recipes are stellar dining events; just indulge in them sparingly. Because recent studies show that butter substitutes are not significantly lower in fat and cholesterol, I do on occasion use real butter, in reduced amounts. Therefore, balance is the key. If you overindulge on one of the marvelously rich recipes within, cut back the next day, or increase your outdoor activity. It will all balance out.

One of the additional benefits of harvesting wild game is the opportunity it gives us to commune with the wild. Interest in wild foods seems to be synonymous with a new interest in embracing the outdoors, in hiking, foraging, and exercising. And cooking with wild game you have harvested yourself is yet another way of getting in tune with nature.

Flavoring Tips

Flavoring wild game and natural foods is one of my favorite parts of writing recipes. I am fascinated by the challenge of selecting the appropriate herbs and spices to enhance each dish. In current and past editions of this book, I have relied heavily on citrus zest. The outer or colored layer of citrus fruits really packs a flavor wallop, and you'll find it called for in dishes from entrées to desserts. Unless specific instructions are given to do something different, always grate zest for use in the recipes in this cookbook.

You may notice that most of the recipes call for little or no salt. This is a personal preference, although a healthful one. Most of us ingest far too much salt through the preservatives that come in almost all prepared and packaged foods. With many studies pointing to salt as one of the major factors in high blood pressure, cutting down on salt in food preparation is a good idea. I urge you to try several of the recipes as written before making a judgment. Many of the natural ingredients and seasonings, like celery and Old Bay Seafood Seasoning, already contain some salt, while many preparations call for fruit juices, garlic, and citrus zest to add extra flavor, making salt unnecessary.

My daughter, Karen, has for years been a food purist, raising most of her own vegetables, and her herb garden is a wonder to behold. I always appreciated her interest and ability in growing and cooking with herbs; however, in recent years I didn't have a garden, and so continued to rely on the dried variety. Since returning to the little house in Benton where I was raised, I, too, have become an herb enthusiast. I have only a small garden, but also a wonderful deck and outdoor living space, where I maintain pots of basil, thyme, rosemary, cilantro (so necessary to my Guatemalan cuisine), oregano, and, as a ground cover in my perennial beds, every mint known to man. This fall, I was unable to do without them, so the bay window in my kitchen is now crowded with pots, and I snip away to my heart's content whenever the stove is on. I have also come to enjoy the healthful and aromatic qualities of fresh gingerroot. Armed with these provisions, I can cook away the day, as the snow swirls just beyond my kitchen window.

Making the Most of Marinades and Sauces

Throughout the book, many recipes call for marinating, because marinades work so well with wild game. In domestic meat, variables of taste have been eliminated through modern farming and feeding techniques. However, wild game varies in flavor depending on its environment and its diet. Marinades serve to level the playing field, giving any game from any area a consistent flavor.

Many of my recipes call for marinating first and then cooking in the same liquid. This gives the flavors of the marinade more of a chance to permeate the meat, continuing to flavor and tenderize it as well. I even go so far as to cool and skim the sauces and use them again. The Chinese have been recycling their rich, flavorful marinades for years, resulting in some enviable culinary secrets. After skimming to remove any fat, I freeze the leftover sauces to use as a starter the next time I prepare that recipe. The starter adds dimension and depth to the new marinade or sauce. This works especially well for the sauce/marinade called for in Chinese Sauced Goose Breasts (see page 105). I never throw that one away, using the leftovers again and again; the sauce tastes better and better every time I reuse it.

I have, of necessity, developed another way to get the most out of marinades. When I prepare the marinade called for in any recipe, I place it, along with the meat, in a sealable plastic freezer bag and freeze it. When I need a good dinner in a hurry, I take the bag out of the freezer the night before and put it in the refrigerator. The meat slowly thaws and marinates all day while the ingredients work their magic. This is my favorite trick. I can make a complicated meal very quickly just by pulling one of these bags out of the freezer.

Large Game

Venison

VENISON IS THE MEAT of any of the antlered members of the deer family—that is, moose, elk, antelope, caribou, mule deer, and white-tailed deer. The whitetail ranges throughout most of the United States, from the southern border of Canada southward through Mexico, Central America, and into South America as far as Peru and Bolivia. Because of this broad geographical distribution, a number of variations in size, color, and habits have developed, and a dozen or more species and subspecies of white-tailed deer are recognized.

The size of a deer depends to a great extent on its environment and its food. The largest white-tailed deer inhabit the northeastern woodlands of the United States and Canada; some of the biggest whitetails on record have been taken in the Adirondack Mountains of New York State and throughout northern New England. Huge bucks weighing as much as 400 pounds have been recorded, with the average weight of a mature male ranging from 250 to 300 pounds. The smallest deer in North America are found in Mexico, where the maximum weight of a mature buck is only about 40 pounds. In the Florida Keys a mature male Key deer rarely exceeds 80 pounds.

Native Americans and Inuit peoples hunted deer long before Europeans settled in the Western Hemisphere. They used its flesh for food and its bones and antlers to fashion crude tools and weapons. Primitive peoples in Europe and Asia used their native deer in similar ways. The Laplanders of northern Europe are still dependent on their reindeer for milk, meat, clothing, housing, and transportation. Possibly because of their reindeer-heavy diet, Laplanders have a low incidence of heart disease and cholesterol problems.

Europeans have long recognized the nutritional and healthful qualities of game. They have feasted since the early ages on the majestic red deer, and have included this animal in their literature and folklore as well as in their cuisine. During the Roman Empire, red deer were farmed in large game preserves with stone walls; fallow deer, a smaller breed, were also popular across the continent, and were prized for the quality and flavor of their meat.

Red deer and fallow deer are now farmed commercially in the United States, along with alligator, buffalo, caribou, ostrich, turtle, and wild boar. Game is raised here in two ways. On deer farms, the animals roam and graze freely and many are provided with shelters, or loafing barns, where they are monitored. The meat from farmed deer is a more uniform product with a consistent taste. Game ranches pasture a larger number of deer on greater acreage, and the deer remain wild in nature. Ranched deer generally come into contact with people only once or twice in their lives. Subsequently, the meat of ranched deer is much closer in flavor to that of wild deer.

A Word on Hunting

Deer have been of great use to man throughout civilization and still represent an important part of our economy. State wildlife bureaus receive a substantial income from the fees charged for hunting licenses, enabling them to support the departments in charge of game management. And the hunting industry is a large employer when you consider all its aspects. The number of workers and services that exist to support the sport of hunting is staggering. Annual expenditures on licenses, guns, transportation, outdoor clothing, camping equipment, lodging, ammunition, food, guides' fees, processing, taxidermy, and fuel amount to millions of dollars. Therefore, wild game is not really "free."

Hunting supports the economy, provides recreation, and keeps us in touch with our heritage. Little wonder it has endured for so many years. Now let's address the biggest benefit of all—good eating!

From Field to Table

To get the most benefit from your venison, you must first consider several things. Most importantly, field dressing and cleanliness must be attended to immediately after the kill. The meat should not be exposed to warm temperatures. Venison, as well as all large game, should cool for at least 36 hours before cooking. Hang your venison in a cool, dark place, protected from insects, with the chest cavity propped open. Both freezing and hanging will age your kill, breaking down the fibers and tenderizing the meat.

The environment, age, and feeding habits of the white-tailed deer greatly affect the flavor of the meat. Deer taken from predominantly forested terrain where the animals have subsisted on browse will generally be stronger in flavor than those taken from farm areas where the deer graze on pasture grasses, apples, and corn. In addition to the relative gaminess of the meat, adjustments in cooking must be made to take into account the age of the animal. Determining the age of a deer is difficult; the most effective way to estimate it is to examine the teeth. Inspect the rear teeth and look for missing teeth or signs of wear on the molars. Deer have a set of baby teeth called milk teeth. At one year, a deer will have his first set of milk teeth. At age one and a half, the first three milk teeth will be worn, but the last three will be sharp, new permanent teeth. At age two, the front teeth will be new, while the permanent teeth in the back will already be showing signs of wear. After three to three and a half years, all permanent teeth will show signs of wear, and deer of this age will require special preparation to tenderize their meat.

In order to help you succeed in the kitchen and enjoy cooking and eating wild game, I have divided the following large game recipes into two categories. Just as preparing a brisket is different from cooking a prime rib, so a young, corn-fed deer raised in rolling hills and fields should be prepared differently from an older, tougher, browse-fed upland animal. For clarity, I have characterized young, tender meat as Type A, and older, tougher, stronger-tasting meat as Type B.

Type A Meat
1. Prepare young, corn-fed deer according to your favorite beef recipes.
2. Prepare young mountain-dwelling deer carefully using my recipes for steaks, rare meat, or roasts.
3. Prepare tender meat using recipes calling for fast, open heat, such as frying, broiling, or pan-frying.

Type B Meat
1. Prepare older meat using slower, moister cooking methods, such as baking in a covered dish, pot roasting, and slow cooking.
2. Avoid cooking older, browse-fed animals with the bone or any fat, as these tend to impart a strong taste. Trim all older meat well to eliminate this effect. In other words, if your meat fits this description and you do not like the "wild" taste of game, do not

use chops, rib steaks, rib roasts, or roasts with the bone in. Consider this when giving your butcher instructions.

Every year, then, your instructions to the butcher will be different, depending on the size, age, and environment of your venison.

After analyzing the diet and age of your deer, give some thought to butchering, even if you plan to have it done professionally. Steaks, chops, and rack roasts can be cut from the ribs or loin and prepared following the recipes in this book. Use the scraps from the extremities, shoulder, and haunch for stew meat or ground meat. Add pork to the ground meat for moistness and flavor, if desired. One part pork to three parts venison is a good proportion to follow.

Field Dressing Large Game

Proper field dressing is important to preserve the quality of the meat. Field dress your game as soon as possible after the kill. All large animals should be eviscerated, skinned, and dried as soon as possible. Prompt evisceration is important because it begins the cooling process and preserves the quality and taste of the meat.

With the animal on its back, prop up the body to keep it supported and steady. Make the first cut into the center of the belly between the hind legs. Cut up to the tip of the breastbone (between the front legs) and down to the anus. After the skin has been opened and pulled back, you are ready to make an incision into the body cavity. Follow the path of the original cut right into and through the body flesh. Pull open the carcass and split the pelvis into two pieces. Tip the split-open animal on its side and empty it of all internal organs. Remove the windpipe, heart, lungs, paunch, and lower organs.

When cutting around the anus, tie it off with some twine before pulling it through the pelvis for removal. Do not let this part of the animal touch any of the meat for fear of contamination, and do not drag it over the meat when removing skin in this area.

Open the breastbone by cutting along the centerline with a heavy knife or hatchet. You can open deer with a knife; larger animals require heavier instruments. Save the liver and heart, if desired. Wipe out the body cavity with clean material (grass or toweling, for example), and prop it open to speed cooling. If you plan to take your animal to a butcher, he or she can skin it for you. Butchering your own game isn't that difficult, and it holds tremendous rewards, but if you feel that you just can't do it, or if time doesn't permit, at least try to skin it yourself.

Plan to skin your kill as soon as possible, to cool down the meat. By doing it yourself you can ensure that there will be no stray hair in the finished product. The skin is also much easier to remove if it is done

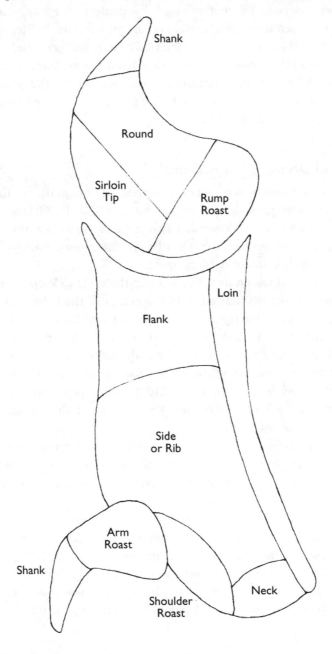

immediately, rather than after the animal has cooled down. Once the skin has been removed, wipe down the carcass using clean towels and fresh water until no hair remains. Being meticulous during this step will pay off every time you dine on venison.

You may choose to wait to skin your animal until you reach home or base camp. However, this often depends on where "home" is. If you are on a hunt far from home in very cold weather, it is not as crucial. However, if you reach home relatively quickly and can skin the animal in the convenience of your garage, there is no need to attempt it in the field, where you may not have water for washing up.

Storing Venison

How many times have we reached into the freezer and pulled out what my family calls mystery meat? It's frustrating trying to figure out what to do with it. When we purchase meat at the store, we expect it to be labeled as to the cut and quality, which determines what we do with it. You would never broil a piece of brisket, for example. We pay more for a prime cut because it will be more tender than a choice quality, which refers to the aging. Give your game the same consideration that you expect at the supermarket. Instruct your butcher to label the packages as to the cut, or do it yourself as you process it.

Packaging is extremely important to the final product. A side of beef purchased from a butcher arrives ready for the freezer, wrapped tightly in heavy freezer-quality paper and labeled. Label all your packages as to the cut, whether they be steaks, chops, rib roast, chuck roast, brisket, tenderloin, eye roast, or sirloin, as that will dictate your cooking method. Don't forget to include the approximate age of the animal, the date packaged, and the type of meat, and you'll have a package that can be prepared successfully. As I indicated earlier, some pieces require moist heat, while others are tender enough to be broiled or roasted. To simplify the explanation of the type of venison you are packaging, I recommend labeling each package Type A or Type B (see page 16). When in doubt, I usually cut off a small steak and fry it up while I'm wrapping the meat. There's nothing like a taste test to tell you for sure.

To preserve moisture and flavor, wrap and freeze whole pieces of steak sections, and wait until just before cooking to slice into steaks. This gives you a fresh, juicy steak that is similar to freshly purchased sirloin of beef.

Perhaps the biggest enemy of frozen food is evaporation caused by frost-free refrigerators. These come equipped with fans and heaters to melt the ice that builds up on freezer shelves, but they also draw moisture from any unsealed package, causing freezer burn. If you are planning to keep any kind of meat for more than six weeks, encase it in a layer of ice. This is simple and easy to do and increases the shelf life by several months. Simply freeze the meat as usual, then remove it from the freezer and unwrap it. Run the frozen meat under a thin stream of cold water, coating all surfaces. As the water hits the frozen meat, it will freeze, encasing the meat in a layer of ice. Refreeze, and repeat the process several times until the ice is several layers thick, effectively sealing the surface of the meat. Rewrap as described above, and you can store your meat for up to nine or ten months with no loss of flavor.

Indian Venison

This is an easy, traditional recipe. European explorers to this continent found Native Americans using this method in the 17th century. Their children also loved to trickle the hot golden syrup onto snow and eat it, as New England children do to this day.

Whether you buy your meat at a grocery store or organic food market, order from a game ranch or farm, or actually harvest a deer, this is a great recipe to involve the children. It's important for them to learn that meat doesn't always come on a plastic tray. Many of us are several generations away from hunting and gathering, but someone is still doing it in order to stock our store shelves and meat cases. Preparing this roast with your children can also be an opportunity to discuss Native American history.

4- to 6-pound venison roast
I cup maple syrup

TYPE B
Marinating time: 2 days

Marinate the roast in the syrup at room temperature for 4 hours. Then cover and refrigerate for 2 days, turning twice a day. Preheat the oven to 250°F. Cook the roast in the syrup, covered, for 3 hours, or until tender.

Serves 4–6

Venison au Naturel

This is my son Scott's special recipe. He whips these steaks up in a flash and likes his rare.

I to 2 pounds venison steaks
I large onion, sliced
I cup hearty red wine
4 tablespoons butter (½ stick)

TYPE A
Marinating time: 4–6 hours

Cover fresh steaks with the red wine and sliced onion and marinate for 4–6 hours. If you are using frozen steaks, you can thaw and marinate them at the same time. Remove the steaks and onions from the marinade and reserve the marinade. In a skillet, melt the butter, then add the steaks and onions and sauté to the desired doneness (see *Note*). Remove the steaks and onions to a heated platter. Heat the reserved marinade, stirring until just boiling. Pour over the steaks and serve.

Note: I find it difficult to judge the doneness of venison; it turns very quickly from rare to well done. If you want rare steaks, give these your undivided attention. Venison cannot be treated like beef. Venison is not marbled with fat, and therefore cooks completely differently. A 1-inch-thick beef steak would need several more minutes of cooking time than is recommended here. I have learned to test venison for doneness by feel. After turning the steaks, begin to push on the surface with your fingers every few seconds. You will be able to feel the flesh firming up as it cooks. With just a little practice, it's possible to catch your venison at just the exact stage of doneness you prefer.

Serves 2–4

Grilled Rosemary Roast

3- to 5-pound venison roast   TYPES A & B
2 to 3 cloves garlic
I tablespoon dried rosemary
Salt and pepper to taste
4 tablespoons butter ($\frac{1}{2}$ stick)
3 tablespoons Worcestershire sauce

Prepare a charcoal fire in a grill with a lid. Spear the roast with an ice pick or sharp knife in six or eight places. Cut each garlic clove into slivers and insert one into each hole. Rub the surface of the meat with the rosemary, salt, and pepper. Using several layers of heavy aluminum foil, make a pan to catch the drippings. When the flames have subsided and the coals are white, place the foil pan on top of the coals (under the grill rack). In a saucepan, melt the butter and add the Worcestershire sauce. Set the roast on the grill rack, and cover. Baste with the butter mixture every 15 or 20 minutes. Grill for 1 hour or more, depending on size. Test for doneness by piercing with a fork. The roast is rare when the juices run red, well done when they are clear.

Serves 4–6

Old-Fashioned Barbecue

This easy recipe takes care of any cuts of game you don't like or don't know what to do with. I used shoulder steaks for this one year. The shoulder steaks were bony, and we didn't care for them at all, so into the slow cooker they went.

I pound venison, any cut   TYPE B
I cup water
I teaspoon oregano
Salt, to taste
2 tablespoons butter
I (16-ounce) bottle *spicy* **ketchup**
Sandwich rolls
Sweet pickle relish (optional)

Place the meat in a slow cooker. Add the water, oregano, and salt to taste. Simmer, covered, on medium heat, until meat falls apart, approximately 1½ hours. Remove the meat with a slotted spoon; discard the broth. Allow the meat to cool, then shred, discarding the fat and bones. Melt the butter in a saucepan. Add the ketchup and blend. Stir in the shredded meat and heat through.

We like this served on buttered, toasted buns and heaped with sweet pickle relish.

Serves 4

Venison Steak Extraordinaire

These steaks look beautiful and are really delicious. Try serving them with an elegant artichoke salad and peas with rice.

½ cup olive oil, plus 2 to 4 tablespoons   TYPE A
   additional oil for frying

¼ cup white wine vinegar

6 to 8 boneless venison steaks, ½ inch thick

2 cups Simple Stuffing (see next page)

I cup Spring Marinara Sauce (see next page)

12 ounces mozzarella cheese, sliced

¼ cup grated Parmesan cheese

Mix ½ cup of the oil with the vinegar. Pour over the steaks and marinate, covered in the refrigerator, for 4–6 hours. Remove the steaks from the marinade. Preheat the oven to 300°F. While the oven is warming, heat 2 tablespoons of oil in a skillet over medium heat. Sauté the steaks in the oil until browned. Add more oil as necessary to keep the steaks from sticking. Remove the browned steaks to a foil-covered baking sheet. Place a pat (about ¼ cup) of stuffing on top of each steak and flatten it. Cover the stuffing with 1–2 tablespoons of marinara sauce, and top with a slice of mozzarella. Sprinkle with the Parmesan cheese. Cover loosely with foil and bake for 1 hour.

Note: This recipe is also delicious made with beef round steaks. You can substitute prepared stuffing mix for the homemade, and a small jar of Italian tomato sauce or marinara sauce serves well if you don't have time to make Spring Marinara Sauce from scratch.

Serves 3–4

Simple Stuffing

8 slices bread, cut into cubes and toasted
1 tablespoon grated onion
2 ribs celery, chopped
2 tablespoons chopped fresh oregano
½ cup hot water
Salt and pepper, to taste

Mix all the ingredients in a bowl until combined. Add more water if necessary to form a moist mixture.

Yield: Approximately 2 cups

Spring Marinara Sauce

This recipe is our favorite marinara. It's low in fat, and very forgiving.

2 tablespoons extra-virgin olive oil
2 tablespoons unsalted butter
3 wild or spring onions, sliced thin
2 cloves garlic, minced
1 (16-ounce) can chopped tomatoes
1 (16-ounce) can whole plum tomatoes, drained and chopped
3 tablespoons tomato paste
2 tablespoons honey
1 teaspoon baking soda
2 tablespoons balsamic vinegar
¼ cup Merlot or other dry red wine

Heat the oil and butter in a large saucepan until blended and warm. Add the onions and garlic, and sauté for 2–3 minutes over medium heat.

Add the tomatoes, tomato paste, and honey. Bring slowly to a simmer, stirring frequently. Simmer for 30–40 minutes. Add the baking soda (it reduces acidity and adds salt); the sauce will bubble up when you add it. Stir it down and add the vinegar and wine. Simmer about 10 minutes more, to allow the flavors to blend.

This sauce is best made a day ahead; it also freezes well.

Note: You can substitute Vidalias or any other onions for the wild ones. Use fresh tomatoes instead of canned, or try adding ½ cup chopped sun-dried tomatoes for more depth of flavor. This sauce goes beautifully over any pasta.

Yield: Approximately 4 cups

Black Diamond Steaks

This easy recipe is an exceptionally rich and delicious dish. It's also elegant made with beef tenderloin. Serve with a green salad.

4 to 6 venison steaks   TYPE A
                                                 Marinating time: 24 hours
Marinade

½ cup canola oil

1 cup hearty red wine

1 medium onion, chopped

¼ cup Dijon mustard

½ teaspoon oregano

¼ teaspoon basil

1 clove garlic, crushed

Place the steaks in a shallow dish. Blend all the marinade ingredients in a blender or food processor. Pour the marinade over the steaks. Marinate in the refrigerator, covered, for 24 hours, turning twice. Remove the steaks from the marinade and grill or broil to the desired doneness. These are best served medium-rare.

Serves 4–6

Steak Normande

This is a dramatic and excellent reduced-fat recipe.

**2 venison round steaks, sliced ¾
inch thick**

**3 tablespoons Dijon mustard
(enough to coat steaks)**

4 tablespoons butter (½ stick)

2 cups sliced fresh mushrooms

½ cup sliced green onions

2 cloves garlic, crushed

2 teaspoons bottled steak sauce

½ cup Cognac

TYPE A
Marinating time: 1 hour

Preheat the broiler.

Coat both sides of the steaks with the mustard and allow to stand at room temperature for one hour. Meanwhile, melt 3 tablespoons of the butter in an ovenproof skillet and sauté the sliced mushrooms in it, stirring frequently. Remove the mushrooms, reserving the mushroom-butter liqueur left in the pan. It should be about ½ cup; if there is more, reduce it by boiling for several minutes. Set aside.

In the same pan, melt the remaining 1 tablespoon butter and sauté the onions and garlic in it. Add the steak sauce, sautéed mushrooms, and reserved mushroom liqueur. Bring the mixture to a boil, then reduce the heat and add the steaks, one at a time. Cook each steak 3 minutes per side, then place the skillet under the broiler for 1 minute. Turn the steaks, and broil for 1 minute more. Immediately remove the steaks from the pan and place on a heated platter. Place the skillet under the broiler again just until the juices return to a boil. Pour the juices over the steaks and drizzle the Cognac over all. Keeping your face away from the dish, ignite the alcohol with a match and serve immediately.

Serves 2

Venison Oriental

This is the recipe that first gave me confidence in the preparation of game. My son Scott didn't know it was venison, and a dinner guest came back the next morning for the recipe. This is easy to prepare and works equally well with beef and pork. Use a bag of frozen Oriental mixed vegetables if you must to shorten preparation time, or vary the vegetable combination to taste.

Marinade *Marinating time: 24 hours*

1 cup oil

¾ cup soy sauce

1 teaspoon dry mustard

2 teaspoons Worcestershire sauce

1 pound venison steak

2 tablespoons sesame oil

1 cup fresh broccoli, chopped

1 medium onion, sliced

1 cup fresh mushrooms, sliced

1 small stalk celery

1 cup shredded green cabbage

½ cup fresh green beans

1 red or green bell pepper, julienned

1 teaspoon grated gingerroot

For the marinade, combine the oil, soy sauce, mustard, and Worcestershire sauce in a jar and shake or combine in a blender. Pour over steak in a shallow dish or sealable plastic bag. Refrigerate for 24 hours, turning once.

Remove the steaks from the marinade, reserving the marinade, and cut into strips, slicing across the grain. Heat the sesame oil in a large skillet or wok and sauté the strips quickly, a few pieces at a time, until browned. Push the pieces to the side of the pan as they are done. When all the steak has been sautéed, remove the strips from the pan.

In the same pan, sauté the broccoli, onions, mushrooms, celery, cabbage, beans, bell peppers, and gingerroot until crisp-tender (about 4–6 minutes). Cover the pan and steam the vegetables 2–3 minutes more. Remove the lid, add the sautéed meat, and stir with the vegetables another 2–3 minutes to reheat. Add some of the reserved marinade to the pan to taste (3–4 tablespoons) and stir well.

Serve over rice or Chinese noodles.

Serves 4

Chinese Pepper Steak

In memory of my friend Ruth Stevenson.

2 tablespoons canola oil   TYPE A
1 teaspoon sesame oil
2 large onions, sliced
2 cups thinly sliced fresh mushrooms
1 or 2 red and/or green bell peppers, sliced
1 clove garlic, crushed
1 ½ pounds venison tenderloin, cut in strips
½ cup beef stock (see page 30)
½ cup cold water
¼ cup soy sauce
½ teaspoon black pepper
½ teaspoon honey
1 teaspoon grated gingerroot
1 tablespoon cornstarch

In a wok or large skillet, heat the canola and sesame oils and sauté the onions, mushrooms, peppers, and garlic until crisp-tender. Remove the vegetables from the pan and add the venison strips. Brown lightly and remove. Add to the pan the stock, water, soy sauce, pepper, honey, gingerroot, and cornstarch, and cook over medium heat until the sauce is smooth and just under a boil. Return the vegetables and meat to the pan and heat through. Serve over rice.

Serves 4–6

Homemade Beef Stock

This rich broth can be used in any recipe calling for beef stock.

1 pound beef, any cut, untrimmed
1 beef soup bone
1 large onion
1 teaspoon salt
1 teaspoon oregano

Cut the beef into 1-inch cubes. Brown the beef in a heavy skillet or kettle over medium heat for at least 30 minutes, stirring frequently. Each piece of beef should be browned, and the pan should take on a dark golden color on the bottom. When the meat is browned and some pieces are just at the point of burning, add 2 cups of water and lower the heat. Stir until you have dislodged all the particles sticking to the bottom of the pan. Add the beef bone, onion, salt, and oregano, and simmer for 30 minutes. With a slotted spoon, remove the meat and onion, leaving the bone in the pot. Boil, uncovered, over medium heat, until the liquid is reduced to 1 cup. Remove the bone. Strain. If not using immediately, freeze for future use.

Yield: 1 cup

Venisonbraten

This is a hearty, flavorful German dish that goes well with buttered noodles on a cold winter night.

Marinade

2 cups water

1 cup red wine vinegar

½ cup cider vinegar

2 medium onions, sliced

½ cup brown sugar

4 bay leaves

½ teaspoon allspice

6 whole peppercorns

½ cup red Burgundy

4- to 6-pound venison roast

1 tablespoon canola oil

Gravy

1 cup meat juices

½ pint sour cream

½ cup broken gingersnaps

TYPES A & B

Marinating time: 4–7 days

In a saucepan, combine all the marinade ingredients except the Burgundy; heat gently, stirring to dissolve the sugar. Remove from the heat and add the Burgundy. Cool. Pour over the roast, cover, and marinate for 4–7 days in the refrigerator, turning twice daily. Remove the meat from the marinade.

In a Dutch oven, heat the oil and brown the meat on all sides, then lower the heat. Strain the marinade and pour over the roast, cover, and simmer on top of the stove over low heat for 2–3 hours, until the meat flakes apart easily with a fork.

To make the gravy, combine the meat juices with the sour cream over low heat. Add the gingersnaps to thicken and heat through.

Note: The roast may also be cooked in the oven, covered, at 200°F for 3–5 hours.

Serves 6

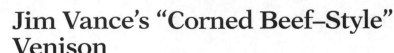

Jim Vance's "Corned Beef–Style" Venison

If you are fortunate enough to have bagged a large game animal that yields a great deal of meat, this recipe will give you some variety in the preparation and taste. Making a corned beef–type roast is fun and interesting. This preparation works well for all large game animals. It will be slightly drier than true corned beef, because of venison's lower fat content.

4- to 6-pound boneless roast   *Marinating time: 7 days*
   (moose, caribou, elk, or venison)

½ pound coarse salt

4 tablespoons brown sugar

I tablespoon pepper

3 bay leaves, crushed

I teaspoon whole cloves, crushed

I teaspoon mace

I teaspoon allspice

I teaspoon garlic powder

½ teaspoon peppercorns, crushed

Clean and trim the roast. Mix together the salt, brown sugar, pepper, bay leaves, cloves, mace, allspice, garlic powder, and peppercorns. Rub the spice mixture into the meat on all sides. Place the roast and any remaining spice mixture in a large plastic freezer bag. Pat the spices into the roast again, shaking the bag to distribute them evenly. Refrigerate for 7 days, turning and rubbing the spices into the meat each day. After the first day, the roast will be marinating in its own juices.

On the seventh day, rinse the roast under cold water and discard the remaining spices. Tie up the roast securely with twine at 3- to 4-inch intervals to prevent it from separating. Place the roast in a large kettle and cover with water. Bring to a boil, then reduce the heat. Simmer, covered, for 5 hours. Remove the pot from the heat, drain off the cooking liquid, and cool the roast. Wrap the meat in foil, place between two boards (cutting boards work well), and set a heavy weight on top of it (a pot of stew or soup makes a good weight). Place the weighted roast in the refrigerator for 12 hours.

To serve, prepare as you would corned beef. Simmer the roast in water with potatoes, carrots, and cabbage, or slice thinly against the grain and serve in sandwiches.

Venison Scaloppine

4 tablespoons olive oil, divided
½ cup dry white wine
1 garlic clove, crushed
1 pound boneless venison, trimmed and cut into steaks
½ cup flour
1 teaspoon paprika
2 cups prepared Spring Marinara Sauce (see page 25)
1 cup thinly sliced mushrooms
3 tablespoons chopped fresh parsley

TYPES A & B
Marinating time: 2–3 hours

Combine 2 tablespoons of the oil with the wine and garlic to make a marinade. Mix well, pour over the prepared meat, and let stand at room temperature for 2–3 hours. Place the flour and paprika in a paper bag and shake to mix. Remove the meat from the marinade and pat it dry. Pound it flat on both sides to tenderize it. Put the meat into the bag of flour and shake to coat. Heat the remaining 2 tablespoons of oil in a skillet and brown the floured meat. Remove the meat from the skillet and drain off the fat. Return the steaks to the skillet, arranging them in a single layer. Pour the Spring Marinara Sauce over the meat and simmer, covered, for 1 hour. Fifteen minutes before serving, add the mushrooms and parsley. Cover the skillet and cook for 15 minutes more. Serve immediately.

Note: This scaloppine can be cooked in half the time using a pressure cooker instead of a skillet. Cooking for 10–12 minutes in the pressure cooker will produce tender, delectable meat.

Serves 4

Tenderloin of Venison Grand Marnier

This is the most elegant, most delicious, most incredible recipe in this book. To me it epitomizes good cooking: Just a few pure ingredients combined with time, love, and patience result in a meal that is a dining experience.

½ cup Grand Marnier
1 orange, cut in half
2 whole venison tenderloins
Canola oil for brushing
Grand Marnier Sauce (see next page)
Fresh parsley for garnish (optional)

TYPE A
Marinating time: 4–5 hours

Place the Grand Marnier in a sealable plastic bag. Cut half of the orange into slices. Remove the zest from the other half and squeeze the juice into the bag. Place the tenderloins in the bag with the liqueur and cover with the orange slices. Seal the bag and marinate in the refrigerator for 4–5 hours.

Preheat the oven to 500°F. Remove the meat from the bag and discard the marinade. Brush all surfaces of the meat with the oil. Place the meat on a rack in an open pan. Insert a meat thermometer into the thickest portion of the largest tenderloin. Place in the oven and immediately reduce the heat to 325°F. Roast until the meat thermometer registers 130°F. The roasting time will vary depending on the size of the tenderloins.

To serve, slice at an angle, cover with Grand Marnier Sauce, and garnish with more orange sections and parsley, if desired.

Note: Use a beef tenderloin if you are not fortunate enough to have venison available.

Serves 4

Grand Marnier Sauce

This is another once- or twice-a-year indulgence. I started to reduce the fat and rework this sauce. But no—let's leave it as written and forget about the fat and calories on this one. Just don't make it every week!

6 tablespoons butter (¾ stick)
2 slices onion
6 tablespoons flour
2½ cups beef stock (see page 30)
½ cup Grand Marnier
Salt and pepper, to taste

Heat the butter in a small, heavy skillet over low heat until browned. Add the onion slices and sauté until light brown. Remove the onions and stir in the flour until well blended. Cook over low heat, stirring constantly, until the flour is a deep mahogany brown, 15–20 minutes. Remove from the heat and gradually stir in the beef stock. Return to the stove and cook over low heat, stirring constantly, until thickened. Remove from the heat and stir in the Grand Marnier. Add salt and pepper to taste.

Note: Make this sauce the day before you cook the venison. It simplifies the preparation, and allows the sauce to ripen in flavor. Heat gently before serving.

Yield: Approximately 3 cups

Venison Potpie

This Pennsylvania Dutch dish is usually served with both a sweet and a sour side dish. Try pepper cabbage and sour green beans for the sour, and apple butter or cottage cheese for the sweet, for an authentic Pennsylvania Dutch supper. Do try the homemade noodles; they really are easy and well worth the extra effort! You'll find the recipe for them in "Down-Home Accompaniments."

2 tablespoons oil   TYPE B

1- to 3-pound venison roast

Salt and pepper, to taste

1 pound dried egg noodles, or homemade noodles (see page 240)

2 large potatoes, peeled and cut into small dice

1 onion, chopped coarsely

1 cup beef stock (see page 30)

1 teaspoon parsley

1 teaspoon oregano

In a heavy pot, heat the oil. Add the roast and brown on all sides. Cover with 1–2 quarts of water; add salt and pepper to taste. Simmer, uncovered, for 2–3 hours. Remove the meat from the pot, reserving the broth. Let the meat cool, then trim and cut into bite-sized pieces. Add the noodles, potatoes, onions, and beef stock to the broth in the pot and simmer until the noodles are cooked. Add the meat, parsley, and oregano, and adjust the seasonings to taste.

Serves 4

Cocktail Meatballs

This is a traditional dish on our Christmas Day buffet table; my daughter Karen still includes it. You can also serve these meatballs as an appetizer.

2 quarts **Spring Marinara Sauce**　　　　　TYPES A & B
　　(see page 25)

I pound **ground venison**

I pound **fresh bulk sausage**

I cup **bread crumbs**

4 **eggs**

½ cup **ketchup**

½ **onion, grated**

½ cup **grated Parmesan cheese**

⅓ cup **sugar**

I or 2 dashes **Worcestershire sauce**

I teaspoon **oregano**

I teaspoon **basil**

I teaspoon **crushed fennel seeds**

I teaspoon **nutmeg**

Bring the Spring Marinara Sauce to a gentle simmer in a large, heavy pot. Meanwhile, combine all the remaining ingredients in a large bowl. Work through the mixture with your hands or a large wooden spoon until well blended. Roll the meat mixture into small meatballs (about 1 inch in diameter), and drop them into the sauce. Should the meatballs feel too soft as you form them, add more bread crumbs. Simmer the meatballs in the sauce for ½ hour. Shake the pot occasionally, but do not stir.

Note: This method makes a hearty sauce, as the juices from the meatballs cook into it, and the meatballs themselves are tender and soft. Eliminating the usual step of browning the meatballs in oil reduces calories and cuts the preparation time in half.

Serves 6–8

Venison Fingers

*My daughter Karen requested this for her wedding reception. I
prepared the recipe the night before the wedding, right up to
sautéing. As the caterer fried the fingers, guests found their way to
the kitchen, following the aroma. We were worried that none of
them would make it to the buffet table. This was an introduction
to wild game for many guests; to the uninitiated, this passes for
very tasty veal.*

Marinade   TYPE A
½ cup olive oil   *Marinating time: 12–24 hours*
¼ cup red wine vinegar
2 teaspoons chopped fresh oregano or 1 teaspoon dried
2 teaspoons chopped fresh basil or 1 teaspoon dried
½ teaspoon salt
1 garlic clove, crushed

1 pound venison steaks
1 cup unseasoned cracker meal
½ cup olive oil

To make the marinade, combine the oil, vinegar, oregano, basil, salt, and
garlic. Set aside. Cut the steaks into finger-sized strips. Place the strips in
a single layer in a glass dish or sealable plastic bag, and cover with the
marinade. Marinate in the refrigerator, covered, overnight, or for 24
hours. (The longer the marinating time, the less wild the flavor.) Remove
the meat from the marinade but do not dry or drain. Dredge the wet
meat in the cracker meal, patting it firmly onto the meat on all sides.
Leaving the meat moist with marinade will make the cracker meal stick
well. In an electric frying pan, heat the oil to 325°F. Sauté the strips in
the oil until golden. Drain on paper towels. Serve hot.

Note: I use the electric frying pan for this recipe because I can con-
trol the heat. You may use any sort of heavy frying pan, as long as you
can maintain the oil at a consistent low temperature.

Serves 4 as an entrée; 6–8 as an appetizer

San Antonio Chili

San Antonio natives swear this is the original American chili. They report that it was developed in the San Antonio jail to accommodate the cheap cuts of tough meat provided the prisoners. Used with venison, this old recipe adapts well, and it is excellent for cuts of older game, such as moose, caribou, and antelope.

½ pound dry red beans
6 cups water
3 tablespoons olive oil
2 pounds venison, cubed
2 cups beef stock (see page 30)
1 can tomato paste
1 red bell pepper, diced
1 green or red chili pepper, diced
3 cloves garlic, grated
3 tablespoons chili powder
1½ tablespoons paprika
1 tablespoon cumin seed
1 teaspoon black pepper
¼ teaspoon salt
¼ teaspoon cayenne pepper

Wash and pick over the red beans. Soak them overnight in 4 cups of water. Heat the oil in a heavy kettle. Add the venison and cook until browned on all sides. Pour off the water from the red beans; combine the red beans and the venison in a slow cooker. Add the beef stock, tomato paste, bell peppers, chilies, garlic, chili powder, paprika, cumin seed, pepper, salt, and cayenne, and stir to combine. Cook on the lowest setting for 6–7 hours, or until the meat falls apart and the beans are tender. Add more water during cooking if necessary. Adjust seasonings to taste, and add more chili peppers if desired.

Serves 6–8 hearty appetites

Variations on San Antonio Chili

The flavors in chili always improve if they are allowed to ripen. Make any of these variations several days prior to serving. Serve with a crusty French bread or a nice loaf of San Francisco's famous sourdough.

1. Go Mexican. Add black olives and chopped green chilies. Serve with corn chips, and pass the hot pepper sauce.
2. Serve on a bed of rice for a complete meal.
3. Add 2 cups chopped mushrooms and some chopped green bell pepper.
4. Turn into a casserole and top with provolone, white American, or mozzarella cheese. Drizzle a little corn syrup on top of the cheese and bake until the cheese melts.
5. Turn it into chili soup by adding 1 quart beef stock and 1 (16-ounce) can tomatoes, or 1 cup tomato juice. Be creative—add mushrooms, alphabet noodles, rice—the possibilities are endless. Check the bottom shelf of the refrigerator. Leftover, cut-up spaghetti is a great addition.

Venison Sausage

THE USUAL WAY to use unwanted cuts of venison is to grind up the leftover scraps and parts for hamburger. But here in Columbia County, we still like good sausage with our eggs, especially on Sunday morning. As the daughter of a butcher, I grew up cranking sausage into a casing, so it is important to me to include directions for making homemade sausage in this book.

Directions for Making Venison Sausage

Meat
1. Trim off the fat and gristle carefully, as they can affect the taste of the finished product.
2. Partially frozen meat will grind more easily than thawed meat.
3. If you are using a food grinder, run some pork fat through it first to grease the worm. The grinder can be cleaned easily by running some bread through at the last.
4. It shortens the process to purchase loose pork sausage already ground at the market to add to your venison.

Casing
1. Purchase a tub of casings at your local market or provision plant.

2. To wash the casings: Thread one end over a faucet; hold the casing in place and let warm water run through it. Cut around or repair any tears or holes by tying them off.

3. Cut the casings into 2- to 3-foot lengths.

4. Soak the casings in warm water for 1 hour.

5. Remove one length of casing at a time. To extract the water, hold one end of the casing with your thumb and forefinger, then pull the length of casing through your fingers, squeezing as it passes between them.

Filling the casing

1. Put the stuffing horn on your food grinder.

2. Thread one end of the casing onto the horn and gradually push on all of the casing, leaving only a 2-inch length hanging.

3. Tie a knot in the hanging end to close the casing for stuffing.

4. Holding the casing on the horn, feed the sausage into the horn. Do not allow any casing to come off the horn until the 2-inch length is firm and full.

5. As you feed the meat through the horn, allow the casing to unroll slowly, making sure it is filled uniformly.

6. Stop filling occasionally to check the uniformity, and pierce any air bubbles with a needle.

7. The sausage should just fill the casing, not stretch it. (Overfilling the casing may cause it to burst during cooking.)

8. To finish filling the last of the casing, remove the horn and casing from the grinder, and poke the remaining sausage in the horn into the casing with the handle of a wooden spoon. Tie the casing to close.

9. Repeat this process with each length of casing until you have used all your venison sausage.

10. Dry your sausages on a rack in a cool room or in the refrigerator for 12 to 24 hours.

Directions for Making Linked Sausages

This is the authentic link sausage that will not come apart during cooking. I learned this procedure in my father's butcher shop.

1. Cut two lengths of cased sausage each about 2 feet long.
2. Hold the lengths of sausage parallel to each other and twist to join the ends.
3. About 4 inches from the joined end, squeeze both pieces to make an indentation in the casing.
4. Lay one piece on top of the other, and again twist to join. You now have one double link.
5. To form the next double link, bring one length of sausage up and through the space between the first links. Pull it through and lay it flat alongside the other piece.
6. Squeeze indentations 4 inches farther down, and repeat twisting and pulling through the hole of the preceding link. When linked in this way, your homemade venison sausage will make a very pleasing display.

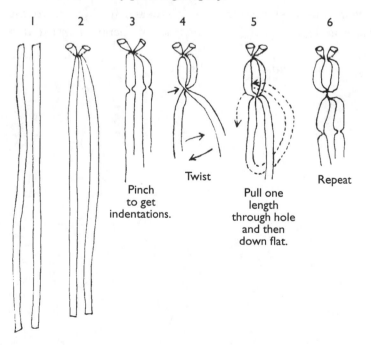

Italian Venison Sausage

This sausage is good in any soup recipe calling for sausage. (I offer several—look for Harvest Soup on page 82.) It is also excellent in Mexican dishes, or in place of hamburger.

5 pounds lean ground venison TYPES A & B

2 pounds ground pork

5 tablespoons sage

4 tablespoons fennel seeds, crushed

3 tablespoons oregano

3 tablespoons basil

3 tablespoons paprika

2 tablespoons salt

2 teaspoons black pepper

2 teaspoons cayenne pepper

1 teaspoon garlic powder, or to taste

Combine all the ingredients in a large bowl and mix as you would for a meat loaf. This moist and spicy sausage can be put in casings if desired.

Note: For best results, freeze sausage uncooked. To make hot sausage, add red pepper sauce and dried red pepper flakes to this recipe.

Yield: 7 pounds; 1 pound serves 4

Mild Sausage

This mild sausage is good for the breakfast table.

I medium onion   TYPES A & B
5 pounds lean ground venison
2 pounds ground pork
5 tablespoons sage
2 tablespoons salt
2 tablespoons cayenne pepper
3 tablespoons lemon juice

Cut the onion into quarters and chop in a blender or food processor.
Combine the venison and pork with the sage, salt, and cayenne, and add
the onion and lemon juice. Put into casings or use as bulk sausage.

Yield: 7 pounds; 1 pound serves 4

Cooking Suggestions for Venison Sausage

1. Cook Italian Venison Sausage in tomato juice, tomato puree, or spaghetti sauce. Bring the liquid to a boil and gently simmer pierced sausages until their juices run clear. The juices will enhance the sauce, and the sauce livens up the sausage.
2. Poach gently in Pheasant Stock (see page 68). Do not pierce the sausages, unless you want them to flavor the broth. The resulting broth may be used as a base for soups.
3. Poach pierced sausages gently in beef stock (see page 30). Serve the stock as consommé for a first course. Float fresh parsley for garnish.
4. Poach in wine or beer. Do not pierce the sausages. Discard the liquid before serving.

Bob Berquist's Venison Sausage

Bob Berquist, an excellent archer, meat cutter, and banker, shares his expertise on the professional preparation of two kinds of venison sausage. "When cutting up the meat, do it with care," Bob advises. "Be sure to remove the tallow (fat) from the deer and the fatty gland located in the middle of each hindquarter. To further preserve the flavor, cut the meat from the bone, rather than cutting through the bones with a meat saw. This keeps the bone marrow from being spread throughout the meat. When grinding the meat for sausage, it is best to use a sausage plate on the grinder. This will give the meat a coarse consistency like that of commercially made sausage." Bob doesn't add pork to venison—this automatically shortens the meat's freezer life, he says, and changes the taste of the meat.

"I hate to leave anything to chance," says Bob, "so I always test each batch of sausage by frying up a few patties immediately. That's half the fun of making sausage at home!" This batch was great; not too hot with spices, yet tangy enough to have your taste buds appreciate the fact that red pepper is included in the ingredients.

4 pounds ground venison   TYPES A & B
4 pounds ground beef
6 tablespoons black pepper
½ tablespoon paprika
1 ¼ teaspoons crushed red pepper flakes

Wet your hands with water and combine the two meats. When they have been mixed thoroughly, wet your hands again and add the pepper, paprika, and red pepper flakes (wet hands prevent the meat from sticking too much).

Yield: 8 pounds

Pure Venison Sausage

The previous recipe and the following sausage variation come from Charlie Burchfield's column "Outdoors Today," which appears in the DuBois, Pennsylvania, Courier-Express. Bob Berquist and Charlie, both successful hunters, enjoy this sausage-making ritual each year.

Bob tells us, "When making sausage with pure venison, you have to reduce the quantity of spices somewhat. Since there is very little fat content to pure venison, a greater percentage of the spices remain in the meat, rather than frying off with the grease."

8 pounds ground venison   TYPES A & B
2 tablespoons black pepper
I tablespoon paprika
I teaspoon crushed red pepper flakes

Proceed exactly as for Bob's original recipe (page 46).

Note: This recipe is most useful for those on restricted diets; it contains very little fat and cholesterol.

Yield: 8 pounds

Other Large Game Recipes

PREPARE CARIBOU, MOOSE, ANTELOPE, and elk the same way you would deer. Any recipe in the chapter on venison will work well. When in doubt as to an animal's age, always use a moist-heat cooking method and marination, or Type B recipes. Prepare young meats as you would beef.

Elk may be aged from 1 to 3 weeks at 34°F, according to taste. Age antelope, caribou, and moose from 3 days to a week. Some connoisseurs of big game contend that freezing takes the place of aging, so you may want to experiment to see what works best for you.

These other large animals can be cut up the same way as deer and beef. And remember, even if you are not a sportsperson, you, too, can experience game. See the "Sources" section for where to order an elk steak.

Elk Roast

This low-fat roast is good with noodles and a green vegetable.

4- to 6-pound elk roast   TYPE B
1 (12-ounce) bottle beer
3 tablespoons steak sauce
6 peppercorns, crushed

Preheat the oven to 250°F. Place the roast in a casserole. Combine the beer, steak sauce, and peppercorns, and pour the mixture over the roast. Cover and bake for 5 hours, basting frequently.

Serves 4–6

Best Elk Steaks Ever

For several years my son Scott hunted the Bob Marshall Wilderness Area in Montana, and he got his first elk there. He grills the steaks and uses the "touch" method to test for doneness (see page 21).

This recipe was inspired by the hot cuisine of the American Southwest. It works well for all red meat. Type A elk, however, needs nothing more than grilling to make an excellent meal. My high school friend Bob Edwards and his wife Ann treated me to elk steaks at their Kalispell, Montana, ranch one summer evening. They were the best I've ever had.

1 (3-ounce) can green chilies, with liquid	TYPE A
	Marinating time: 4–6 hours
1 (12-ounce) bottle stout (or any other dark beer)	
1 to 2 pounds elk steaks	
1 green bell pepper, chopped	
4 to 6 green onions, thinly sliced	
2 tablespoons olive oil	
Hot pepper sauce, to taste	

To make the marinade, combine the liquid from the can of green chilies with the stout. Pour over the steaks and marinate at room temperature for 4–6 hours. Preheat the broiler. Sauté the green pepper and onions in the oil. Add the green chilies and hot pepper sauce to taste. Remove the steaks from the marinade and broil to the desired doneness. Top with the green pepper mixture, then run under the broiler until the topping is sizzling.

Serves 4–6

Elk Burgundy

This dish is naturally low in fat.

4- to 6-pound elk roast
1 cup red Burgundy
1 large onion, sliced
2 cloves garlic, minced
½ teaspoon rosemary
½ teaspoon thyme
6 peppercorns, crushed
Salt, to taste

TYPE B
Marinating time: overnight

Combine all ingredients in a sealable plastic bag or covered container and marinate overnight in the refrigerator. Preheat the oven to 300°F. Turn the meat and place with the marinade in a covered casserole. Bake for 2 hours, turning twice.

Serves 4–6

Elk Stroganoff

Homemade noodles make this dish extra special.

1 ½ pounds elk round steak	TYPES A & B

¼ cup flour

¼ cup pepper

2 tablespoons olive oil

2 tablespoons butter

1 medium onion, chopped

1 clove garlic, chopped

2 cups sliced mushrooms

2 cups venison or beef stock (see page 30)

½ cup sour cream

½ cup plain yogurt

Homemade noodles (see page 240)

Cut the steak into strips, then into pieces about 2 inches long. Combine the flour and pepper and dredge each strip in the mixture. Heat the oil and butter in a heavy skillet. Add the onions and garlic and stir until the garlic is golden. Push the onions and garlic to the side of the pan. Add the floured meat and sauté quickly to brown on all sides. Remove the meat from the pan. Add the mushrooms to the pan and sauté, stirring constantly, for 10 minutes. Lower the heat and add the venison or beef stock, sour cream, and yogurt. Stir until well blended. Return the meat to the pan and heat through (3–4 minutes).

Serve over homemade noodles.

Serves 4

Roast Caribou

This savory low-fat recipe can also be prepared with beef,
venison, or elk.

I cup hearty red wine, divided
I garlic clove, crushed
3- to 4-pound caribou roast
I teaspoon meat tenderizer
I cup whole-berry cranberry sauce
¼ cup honey
I lemon, sliced

TYPE B
Marinating time: 24 hours

Combine ½ cup of the wine and ½ cup water with the garlic. Pour over
the meat, place in a sealable plastic bag or sealed covered container, and
marinate overnight in the refrigerator.

Preheat the oven to 275°F. Apply the meat tenderizer to the outside
of the roast. Place in an open roasting pan and roast for 2 hours. Meanwhile, melt the cranberry sauce and honey in a double boiler or over low
heat. Remove from the heat, add the remaining ½ cup of wine, and stir
to blend. Use this mixture to baste the roast frequently. After 2 hours of
roasting time, top the roast with the lemon slices and return to the oven
for 2–3 hours more, continuing to baste. The roast is done when the
juices run clear.

Serves 4–6

Spanish Caribou

½ cup flour

½ teaspoon oregano

Salt and pepper, to taste

1- to 1½-pound caribou round steak

2 tablespoons butter

2 tablespoons light olive oil

1 (10½-ounce) can tomato soup, or 2 cups finely chopped
   ripe tomatoes

1 medium onion, sliced

1 green bell pepper, sliced into rings

1 (10-ounce) can chopped green chilies

Combine the flour, oregano, salt, and pepper. Dredge the steak in the seasoned flour. Heat the butter and oil in a frying pan and brown the steak. Cover with the tomato soup or chopped tomatoes, onion, and green peppers. Cover the pan, lower the heat to a slow simmer, and cook for 1–1½ hours. Using a fork, check for doneness: The caribou should flake apart. Top with the chopped chilies and run under the broiler for a few minutes.

Serve on a platter with some of the pan drippings ladled over the top.

Serves 4

Moose Roast

¼ cup flour   TYPE B

1 teaspoon paprika

½ teaspoon oregano

4-pound moose roast

2 tablespoons butter

2 tablespoons oil

1½ cups tomato juice

½ teaspoon garlic powder or 1 garlic clove, crushed

4 carrots, sliced

3 onions, chopped

1 cup chopped celery

Mix the flour, paprika, and oregano. Dredge the meat in this mixture to coat on all sides. Heat the butter and oil in a heavy kettle. Brown the roast on all sides. Add the tomato juice and garlic and simmer, covered, for 2–3 hours. Add the carrots, onions, and celery and cook for ½ hour more, or until the vegetables are tender. Serve with pot juices.

Serves 6–8

Moose Swiss Steak

2 pounds moose round steak
½ cup hearty red wine
I onion, sliced
½ cup flour
½ teaspoon paprika
2 tablespoons oil
I cup diced celery
I (16-ounce) can tomatoes, drained, or 2 cups chopped fresh tomatoes
I tablespoon Worcestershire sauce
2 teaspoons cornstarch

TYPE B
Marinating time: 4 hours

Marinate the steaks in the wine and sliced onion in the refrigerator for at least 4 hours. Preheat the oven to 250°F. Pat the steaks dry and dredge in a mixture of the flour and paprika. In a Dutch oven, heat the oil, add the steaks, and brown on both sides. Add the celery, tomatoes, and Worcestershire sauce, cover tightly, and cook in the preheated oven for 2 hours. Remove the roast to a platter and keep warm.

Dissolve the cornstarch in 1 cup of water and stir into the pan juices. Heat gently on the stove top until thickened into gravy. Pour the gravy over the roast to serve.

Serves 4–6

Mexican Moose

This is delicious with tortilla chips and an avocado salad.

2 green bell peppers, chopped
1 cup chopped onions
3 tablespoons oil
2 cloves garlic, crushed
2 pounds ground moose
8 bay leaves
2 cups beef stock (see page 30)
1 cup white rice

Sauté the peppers and onions in the oil until the onions become translucent and the peppers soften. Add the garlic and sauté for 2–3 minutes more. Add the ground moose and cook over medium heat, stirring, until browned. Add the bay leaves and simmer, covered, for ½ hour.

Meanwhile, bring the beef stock to a boil. Add the rice, lower the heat, and cover. Simmer 10–15 minutes, or until all the stock is absorbed by the rice and each kernel is tender.

Remove the bay leaves from the meat mixture. Combine the meat mixture with the rice. Simmer for 5 minutes to combine the flavors.

Note: Never serve anything with whole bay leaves still in it. The stems of these dried leaves can puncture intestines and cause a great deal of distress. If you cannot remove the leaves before serving, break off the leaf away from the center vein and crumble just the leaf into the food, discarding the stem.

Serves 4–6

Moose Stew

This stew always reminds me of a huge shadow that followed us on a moonlight walk through a Maine campground—a big moose leisurely strolling along behind us!

3 tablespoons oil   TYPE B

1 pound moose stew meat, trimmed and
   cut into cubes

4 medium potatoes, diced

3 ribs celery, diced

1 medium onion, chopped

6 medium carrots, sliced

1 (16-ounce) can stewed chopped tomatoes

1 (10½-ounce) can tomato soup

1 cup beef stock (see page 30)

1 teaspoon basil

1 teaspoon paprika

1 teaspoon ground black pepper

1 garlic clove, crushed

In a large stew pot, brown the meat cubes in the oil. Add the remaining ingredients and simmer, covered, on top of the stove for 2 hours. Or cook in a slow cooker on medium heat for 5–6 hours.

Serves 4

Hearty Prospector's
Antelope Stew

TYPE B

¼ cup flour

½ teaspoon salt

½ teaspoon cayenne pepper

½ teaspoon black pepper

2 pounds antelope stew meat, cut into 1-inch cubes

½ cup olive oil, divided

3 medium onions, sliced

1 cup chopped celery

2 cloves garlic, crushed

1 (12-ounce) bottle dark beer

1 tablespoon soy sauce

1 tablespoon steak sauce

1 tablespoon Worcestershire sauce

2 bay leaves

½ teaspoon thyme

3 tablespoons chopped fresh parsley

1 tablespoon honey

6 carrots, thinly sliced

6 medium potatoes, peeled and quartered

1 (10-ounce) package frozen peas

Combine the flour, salt, and both peppers. Put in a plastic or paper bag and add 1 cup of antelope cubes at a time. Toss and pat to coat all pieces well. Repeat until all the meat is coated with the flour mixture. Set aside. Heat ¼ cup of the oil in a heavy skillet; sauté the onions, celery, and garlic. Remove the vegetables from the pan and add the remaining ½ cup oil. Sauté the meat until browned on all sides. Return the onions, celery, and garlic to the pan and add the beer, soy sauce, steak sauce, Worcestershire sauce, bay leaves, thyme, and parsley. Bring the mixture to a boil. Add the honey and stir to combine. Cover, reduce the heat, and simmer for 2 hours. Or cook in a slow cooker on the low setting for 3–4 hours.

Shortly before you are ready to serve the stew, cook the carrots, potatoes, and peas in a microwave or on the stove top. When the meat is tender, remove the bay leaves, add the cooked vegetables and heat through. This method keeps the vegetables brightly colored, crisp, and fresh tasting, instead of being "cooked to death" with the rest of the stew.

Note: If your antelope is old, or known to be tough, increase the cooking time by ½ hour.

Serves 4–6

Bear

FIELD DRESS BEAR in the same manner as you would a deer. Do not drag the animal if you want to save the hide. Because the bear is such a heavy animal, when setting out for a bear hunt, be prepared with special equipment to field dress it. You'll need a hoist, meat sacks, blankets or canvas, and lots of ground black pepper. Hang the animal and quarter the meat, storing it in sacks to keep it clean. Dry meat stays clean and bacteria-free, so make sure the meat is dry and free of flies. Should blowflies appear, rub pepper into the surface of the meat and dry the area in the sun.

Bear meat can be aged from 3 to 7 days. Aging enables the enzymes in the meat to tenderize it and improve the flavor. Fluctuation in temperature causes moisture to form on the meat, and moisture hastens the formation of bacteria, so whatever your plans for your meat, make sure the temperature is constant.

Meat from a young bear (1 or 2 years old) is delicious. Prepare it as you would pork, using any moist-heat recipe. Bear and sauerkraut, barbecued bear, and bear "pigs-in-blankets" are all excellent choices. Slow cookers work well with bear. I include several recipes just to get you introduced to the sweet goodness of the meat. After you try these, strike out on your own and experiment, using your favorite beef recipes or any of the venison recipes in this book.

Bear Pot Roast

Marinade *Marinating time: 24 hours*
4 cups red wine
1 medium onion, sliced
2 bay leaves
½ teaspoon rosemary
4 to 6 black peppercorns, crushed

3- to 4-pound bear roast
Oil for browning

To make the marinade, combine the wine, onions, bay leaves, rosemary, and crushed peppercorns. Place the roast in a deep bowl or sealable plastic bag and pour the marinade over it. Refrigerate overnight, turning every 6 hours to make sure all the sides have been marinated. Before cooking, remove the roast from the marinade and pat dry, reserving the marinade. Preheat the oven to 250°F. Heat the oil in a heavy Dutch oven and brown the meat lightly on all sides. Cover and bake for 1 hour per pound of meat, basting several times with the marinade during roasting.

Serves 4

Old English Bear Sandwiches

I recipe Roast of Bear (see page 63)
I cup beef stock (see page 30)
Hard sandwich rolls, toasted
Horseradish, to taste
Hot peppers, to taste

Preheat the oven to 375°F. Meanwhile, keep the stock hot in a saucepan. Slice the roast of bear very thinly with an electric knife or using a meat slicer. Heap the meat onto the rolls and wrap in foil. Place in the oven for 5 minutes to warm the meat. To serve, hold the roll sideways and pour the hot stock through the meat. Serve with horseradish and hot peppers, if desired.

Note: Use your own homemade beef stock, or save the juice from a beef roast and freeze. These natural beef juices give the finishing touch to this sandwich. Canned beef broth may also be used.

Serves 4

Roast of Bear

Marinade
2 cups venison or beef stock
I large onion, sliced thin
I teaspoon paprika
½ teaspoon salt
½ teaspoon basil
½ teaspoon oregano

Marinating time: 4 hours
to overnight

4- to 6-pound bear roast

Combine the marinade ingredients in a deep bowl or sealable plastic bag and pour over the roast. Cover and marinate for at least 4 hours, turning twice. (A frozen roast can be marinated overnight in the refrigerator while thawing.) Put the roast, along with the marinade, in a slow cooker or Dutch oven, and cover tightly. Cook on the lowest setting in the slow cooker (or bake in the Dutch oven at 275°F) for 1 hour per pound of meat, or until tender. Turn the roast several times during cooking. A tight-fitting lid is essential for this roast in order to tenderize the meat and enhance the flavor.

Serves 4

Bear Meat Jerky

This recipe works equally well with venison.

**1 pound or more bear meat (preferably
   hindquarter, or other tender cuts)**
1 quart warm water
1 cup salt
2 to 3 cups Liquid Smoke (see *Note*)
Black pepper, to taste

Cut the meat into slices 1¼ inches thick. Freeze slightly for easier handling. Cut each slice into ¼-inch-thick strips. Soak in a mixture of water, salt, and Liquid Smoke for 10 minutes. Sprinkle with pepper to taste. Drain well. Place the strips directly on oven racks, being careful not to overlap strips. Turn the oven to its lowest setting and bake for 3 hours. Turn off the heat, and let the meat stand in the oven until all the heat has gone. Store in airtight jars.

Note: Liquid Smoke is a seasoning that can be found in most supermarkets in the condiment section. Most brands contain water, natural hickory smoke flavor, vinegar, and molasses.

Serves 6–8 as a snack

Fowl and Small Game

Fowl

UPLAND GAME BIRDS are ground-dwelling. Their food consists mainly of insects, berries, and wild grains. They are excellent insect-controllers and are valued by farmers and country folk. Game birds can be found in every environment our country has to offer, from the marshes of the East and South to the prairies and deserts of the West, and in all the forests in between.

The fall hunting season for game birds is a blessing and a carefully designed plan for wildlife management in all sections of our country. Because upland game birds are not migratory, many would die a slow and pitiful death of starvation were it not for the fall harvest.

The pheasant is a close relative to the domestic chicken and can be prepared in a similar fashion. Ring-necked pheasants, natives of China, were brought to this country in 1881. They took to their new habitat with great adaptability and have thrived and multiplied ever since. They are especially numerous near the grain farms of the Great Plains. The ring-neck is perhaps the least wild-flavored of all the game birds; the flesh is mild and all white meat except for the legs.

The age of the bird is an important consideration. In general, young birds will have short, round claws; older birds will have developed longer, sharp claws. Young birds and organically raised fowl may be roasted or broiled and used in any fowl recipe, with no special preparation necessary. Older birds—which you can expect to be tougher—should be braised or stewed. If you want to roast an older bird, use meat tenderizer to condition it. A flavored tenderizer will further minimize the wild taste. The older the bird, the longer it should stand with the tenderizer applied. Marinades of wine or citrus juice may also be used. A large bird, such as wild turkey, benefits from tenderizing in the refrigerator for 12 to 24 hours. Apply the tenderizer to the cavity, and rub under the skin of the breast.

Fish-eating fowl have rich dark meat that is almost always fishy tasting. Using only the breast meat and marinating it at least 24 hours in vinegar and salt will minimize this problem. Use 2 cups of vinegar with 4 tablespoons of salt for the marinade. You may also use tenderizer on these birds after marinating them. Wash and dry the fowl before cooking. An apple, quartered and placed in the cavity, also absorbs some of the fishy taste. To estimate the number of birds you will need for the number of people you are serving, follow these suggestions:

1 grouse will serve 1 person.
1 partridge will serve 1–2 depending on size.
1 pheasant will serve 2–4 depending on size.
Partridge, grouse, and pheasant are similar in taste and texture. Recipes for pheasant may be used with partridge and grouse with equal success.

From Field to Table

Successful cooking of game birds depends on several things: their condition, their age, and proper handling in the field. Take care to transport your game home in the best possible condition. Pay extra attention on warm days, because every hour in the field without refrigeration will seriously affect the quality of your bird.

Take a cooler and a block of ice along if the weather is warm. Your cleaned fowl can then be iced down as soon as you get back to your car. Eviscerate them immediately and take time for thorough cleaning—these procedures help to preserve all the delicate flavors.

Should you be caught far afield with no provisions to cool down game birds, use a basket lined with leaves or moss and moistened in an effective way to protect them if the day is breezy. Under no circumstances should you carry several birds all day in a hunting-coat pouch near your body. Carrying game in this manner will render it inedible.

After the field-dressed bird has arrived in the kitchen, wash it thoroughly in cold running water. Remove the pin feathers and the kidney and lung tissues on either side of the backbone. Cut off the oil sac at the back. Wash again, rinsing the inside of the bird well. Next, remove the feet and leg tendons, then make an incision down the center of the neck skin, so that the skin may be pulled away. Remove the neck by cutting it off close to the body. Remove the crop and windpipe from this opening. Wash the bird one more time and refrigerate.

Your game bird is now ready for the pot or the freezer. Be sure to date the packages, and to indicate whether the bird is young or mature.

Cutting up Game Birds

Game birds can be cut apart as you would a chicken. They tend to have thicker bones and skin than a domestic chicken, so use a sharp, serrated knife or heavy poultry shears. Be sure to remove the oil sacs on either side of the bird's spine before cooking.

Cut 1. Move leg back and forth to locate joint. Make the cut as indicated through the skin. Continuing to move the leg, cut the leg from the body and right through the joint. After the meat has been severed, bend the leg away from you and down. This will cause the thigh joint to appear, making cutting through it easy.

Cut 2. Repeat with the other leg.

Cut 3. Cut down the center of the breast and spread the bird apart. Rinse the cavity and clean again, picking away organs or entrails and discarding.

Cut 4. Using the bird's skeleton as a guide, cut breasts away from the backbone.

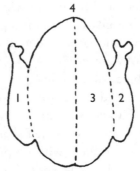

Pheasant Stock

If you use the recipes in this book calling for the breast meat of pheasant, the remaining pheasant pieces will make a good stock.

3 tablespoons oil
1 pound pheasant pieces (necks, backs, legs, and wings)
Water (about 1 quart)
Salt and pepper, to taste

Heat the oil in a heavy pot over medium heat. Add a few pieces of pheasant at a time and brown. Push aside the browned pieces and repeat until all the pieces have been browned and the pot has a golden crust. Scrape up browned bits and cover the meat and bones with water. Cover and simmer for 2 hours.

Remove the meat and bones from the pot and discard. Strain the stock for use in soups and sauces. Season with salt and pepper to taste. This recipe may be doubled or even tripled. The stock freezes well.

Note: Meat scraps may be picked from the bones and included in soups. You can use this technique for any type of fowl.

English Baked Pheasant

2 pheasants, skin on   *Marinating time: 2 hours*
2 cups ale or beer
1 ½ cups Italian seasoned bread crumbs
2 eggs, beaten
1 teaspoon paprika

Cut the unskinned pheasants into serving-sized pieces. Arrange the pieces in a deep dish or a sealable plastic bag. Pour the ale over the pieces and marinate for 2 hours at room temperature. Remove the pieces from the marinade. Preheat the oven to 350°F. Place the bread crumbs in a bowl or plastic bag and dredge the pheasant pieces in them. Dip each pheasant piece in the beaten egg, and then dredge again with bread crumbs and sprinkle generously with paprika. Arrange on a baking sheet or in a baking dish. Bake for 1 hour.

Serves 4

Spiced Pheasant Breasts

This recipe makes a low-fat—and delicious—meal.

3 or 4 pheasant breasts, split   *Marinating time: 5–6 hours*
6 tablespoons soy sauce
4 garlic cloves, minced fine
1 teaspoon cinnamon
4 thin slices gingerroot
½ teaspoon nutmeg
¼ cup lemon juice

Place the pheasant breasts in a sealable plastic bag or baking dish. Combine the soy sauce, garlic, cinnamon, gingerroot, nutmeg, and lemon juice in a blender and blend until smooth. Pour over the pheasant, cover, and refrigerate 3–4 hours to marinate. Remove from the refrigerator and allow to stand for 1–2 more hours before baking. Preheat the oven to 300°F. Bake the breasts in the marinade, flesh-side down, covered, for 1–1½ hours, depending on the size of the birds. The breasts are done when the juices run clear.

Serves 2–3

Rolled Pheasant Breasts in Mushroom Wine Sauce

Try this beautiful and elegant entrée with a capon, or any organic fowl.

3 tablespoons butter
½ cup chopped onions
¼ cup sliced green onions, including green tops
1 cup sliced mushrooms
¼ teaspoon cayenne pepper
5 whole pheasant breasts
½ cup dry vermouth
½ cup chicken or pheasant stock (see page 68)
2 tablespoons cornstarch
¼ cup water

In a heavy skillet, melt the butter. Sauté the onions and mushrooms until lightly browned. Sprinkle with the cayenne, then remove the onions and mushrooms with a slotted spoon and allow to cool. Cut the pheasant breasts in half and debone. Pound the breasts lightly to flatten them. Spread the breasts with the mushroom mixture, then roll up and fasten with string or poultry pins. In the skillet, brown the breasts on all sides, adding more butter if necessary. Pour the vermouth and stock into the pan, cover, and simmer for 30–35 minutes, or until the breasts are tender. Add water if the pan becomes dry. Remove the breasts to a platter. Add the cornstarch to the ¼ cup of water and stir until blended. Pour into the pan and scrape up any browned particles. Stir over medium heat until a smooth sauce forms. Return the breasts to the pan. Reheat and serve.

Serves 4

Pheasant Breasts Margarita

This recipe can be made using almost any type of fowl or small game, including wild turkey, duck, rabbit, quail, Cornish game hen, and chicken.

4 tablespoons flour
½ teaspoon paprika
⅛ teaspoon ground ginger
4 to 6 pheasant breasts, boned
2 tablespoons peanut oil
¼ cup tequila, 80 proof
Margarita Sauce (see next page)

Combine the flour, paprika, and ginger. Pound the spice mixture into the pheasant breasts until they are coated and flattened slightly. Heat the oil in a skillet and sauté the breasts until they are browned on both sides, 6–8 minutes, or until the juices run almost clear. Sprinkle with the tequila and, leaning away from the pan, light with a match. Cook for 2 minutes more, add the Margarita Sauce, and heat through.

Serves 4

Margarita Sauce

2 cloves garlic, minced

4 green onions, chopped

1 tablespoon olive oil

1 cup pheasant stock, divided (see page 68)

2 tablespoons lime juice

1 teaspoon Dijon mustard

1 tablespoon minced fresh parsley

½ teaspoon basil

½ teaspoon oregano

1 tablespoon flour

In a saucepan, sauté the garlic and onions in the oil until golden. Add ½ cup of the stock. Stir in the lime juice, mustard, parsley, basil, and oregano and heat to simmering. In a separate bowl, whisk the flour into the remaining ½ cup of stock. Slowly stir into simmering broth mixture until thickened and smooth.

Broccoli and Pheasant Casserole

When kids move away, one of the things they miss most is Mom's home cooking. I haunt flea markets and garage sales for small baking dishes that are in good condition and can be sterilized. Whenever I make something the kids would enjoy, I double the recipe and fill a casserole, tape the recipe to the top, and freeze. This makes a loving care package to send away with them the next time they visit, and they can add a dish to their cupboards as well as a recipe to their file.

6 whole pheasant breasts

2 (10-ounce) packages frozen chopped broccoli

1 cup plain yogurt

2 teaspoons lemon juice

1 teaspoon chicken bouillon

½ teaspoon lemon zest

1 cup Spicy Italian Salad Dressing (see next page)

**1¼ cups grated fontina cheese
   (sharp cheddar may be substituted)**

½ cup bread crumbs

Gently poach the pheasant breasts in 4 cups of water until the juices run clear, 20–30 minutes. Remove the breasts, reserving the broth for later use in soups, sauces, and gravies. Meanwhile, cook and drain the broccoli. Preheat the oven to 300°F. Coat a baking dish with cooking spray and place the broccoli in an even layer over the bottom of the dish. Split the pheasant breasts by cutting them in half. Place the split breasts on top of the broccoli. Mix the yogurt, lemon juice, bouillon, zest, salad dressing, and ¼ cup of the cheese. Pour over the pheasant to cover. Sprinkle the remaining 1 cup of cheese over the top of the casserole, and top with the bread crumbs. Bake, uncovered, for 30 minutes, or until bubbling and heated through.

Note: This is a very easy casserole to make ahead. Refrigerate overnight, then bake just before serving.

Serves 6

Spicy Italian Salad Dressing

⅔ **cup salad oil**
¼ **cup red wine vinegar**
2 cloves garlic, minced
½ **teaspoon grated onion**
½ **teaspoon oregano**
½ **teaspoon Old Bay Seafood Seasoning**
Dash hot pepper sauce

Combine all ingredients until thoroughly blended.

Yield: 1 cup

Sunchoke Pheasant

This elegant dish is quick and easy to prepare.

6 pheasant breasts
1 pound Jerusalem artichokes, cut into ½**-inch slices**
12 ounces frozen pearl onions
Paprika, to taste
Garlic powder, to taste
Salt and pepper, to taste
2 cups orange juice

Preheat the oven to 325°F. Place the pheasant breasts, Jerusalem artichokes, and onions in an ovenproof dish. Sprinkle on the paprika, garlic powder, and salt and pepper, pour the orange juice over them, and bake for 1 hour.

Serves 4

Pheasant Moo Goo Gai Pan

Serve this pleasing low-fat preparation over brown rice.

I pound boned pheasant breasts
I teaspoon sesame oil
I ½ tablespoons soy sauce
I teaspoon grated gingerroot
I teaspoon light olive oil
½ cup chopped green onions
½ cup minced celery
I cup thinly sliced mushrooms
I clove garlic, crushed
I cup pheasant or chicken stock, divided (see page 68)
I (10-ounce) package frozen Oriental mixed vegetables,
   partially thawed
I teaspoon cornstarch

Cut the pheasant breasts into 1-inch cubes and combine with the sesame oil. Add the soy sauce and gingerroot. Stir to mix well.

Heat the olive oil in a wok. Stir-fry the pheasant in small batches over high heat until the meat is lightly browned. Push the meat to one side and add the green onions, celery, mushrooms, and garlic. Stir-fry until the celery is crisp-tender and the onion is translucent, about 3–4 minutes. Stir in ½ cup of the stock and the Oriental vegetables. Cover and steam for 4–5 minutes. Meanwhile, stir the cornstarch into the remaining ½ cup of stock until smooth; add to the wok. Cook, uncovered, and stir until the sauce is thick and the ingredients well mixed.

Note: If you don't have a wok, this dish can be made in a large skillet with a lid.

Serves 4

Pheasant Madrid

This is an unusual, well-seasoned way to cook fowl.

2 teaspoons garlic powder   *Marinating time: 2–3 hours*
1 teaspoon paprika
½ teaspoon oregano
½ teaspoon cinnamon
2 or 3 pheasants, split in half
4 cups hot and spicy tomato juice
1 medium onion, diced
1 lemon, zest removed and reserved, sliced
1 bay leaf

Combine the garlic powder, paprika, oregano, and cinnamon, and rub into all surfaces of the pheasant halves. Place the pheasant halves flesh-side down in a baking dish and pour the tomato juice over them. Sprinkle with the onions and cover with the lemon slices. Sprinkle evenly with the reserved lemon zest. Add the bay leaf to the baking dish. Marinate at room temperature for 2–3 hours.

Preheat the oven to 300°F, then bake the pheasants in the marinade for 1–1½ hours, depending on the size of the pheasants. Test for doneness by moving a leg. If it moves freely in the joint, the bird is cooked. Discard the bay leaf before serving.

Serves 4–6

Hungarian Pheasant Breast Paprikash

2 tablespoons butter

1 onion, chopped

1 tablespoon paprika, plus more for garnish

1 tablespoon black pepper

4 pheasant breasts, cleaned and split

1 ½ cups pheasant or chicken stock (see page 68)

½ pint yogurt, drained (see *Note*)

¼ cup chopped green onions

1 clove garlic, minced

¼ teaspoon Worcestershire sauce

½ cup cream

Melt the butter in an electric skillet and sauté the onion until soft. Add the paprika, pepper, and pheasant breasts. Brown the breasts for 8–10 minutes, or until the breast meat is tender. (The younger the bird, the less cooking time necessary.) Remove the pheasant breasts to a warm serving platter. Add the pheasant stock and the drained yogurt to the pan, scraping to include the drippings. Add the green onions, garlic, and Worcestershire sauce. Mix well and heat through, stirring constantly. Add the cream and blend. Pour the sauce over the pheasant breasts and sprinkle with paprika. Serve immediately.

Note: To drain yogurt, place in a strainer lined with cheesecloth and drain in the refrigerator for 1–2 hours. This is a great substitute for sour cream.

Serves 4–6

Elegant Pheasant

Marinade   *Marinating time: 3 days*

⅔ cup oil

¼ cup white wine vinegar

2 tablespoons water

2 tablespoons finely grated onion

I clove garlic, minced

½ teaspoon red pepper flakes

½ teaspoon oregano

¼ teaspoon basil

¼ teaspoon sugar

¼ teaspoon salt

4 to 6 cleaned and boned pheasant breasts

I cup Italian seasoned bread crumbs

2 eggs, beaten with 2 tablespoons water

4 tablespoons butter (½ stick)

½ cup olive oil

Combine all the marinade ingredients in a jar and shake to blend. Put the pheasant breasts in a covered container or sealable plastic bag and pour the marinade over them. Refrigerate and marinate for at least 3 days, turning twice daily. Remove the breasts from the marinade, but do not dry or drain. Dredge the wet breasts in the bread crumbs. Dip the breasts in the beaten egg mixture, then in the crumbs again. The dish can be prepared up to this point ahead of time and then refrigerated until ready to cook.

Melt the butter in an electric frying pan (see *Note*, page 80) and add the olive oil. Increase the temperature to 350°F and sauté the breasts until golden. Drain on paper towels. This dish can be held in a warm oven, uncovered, for up to ½ hour before serving.

Note: Packaged Italian salad dressing mix, prepared according to package instructions, may be substituted for the marinade.

Serves 4

Fried Pheasant

Marinade   *Marinating time: overnight, or up to 2 days*

½ cup olive oil

¼ cup white wine vinegar

1 clove garlic, crushed

1 teaspoon chopped fresh basil

1 teaspoon chopped fresh parsley

1 teaspoon chopped fresh oregano, or ½ teaspoon dried

1 pheasant, cut into serving-size pieces

1 cup seasoned cracker meal

¾ cup olive oil

Combine the marinade ingredients. Arrange the pheasant pieces in a bowl or in a sealable plastic bag and cover with the marinade. Cover and refrigerate overnight, or for up to 2 days. Remove the pheasant from the marinade but do not dry or drain it. Dredge the wet pieces in the cracker meal. Pat the meal firmly into the fowl on all sides. Discard the marinade, or freeze for reuse.

Bring the oil to 325°F in an electric frying pan (see *Note*). Fry the pheasant pieces until golden and drain on paper towels. Serve hot.

Note: An electric frying pan allows you to maintain an even heat while frying; however, a regular skillet on the stove top will work just as well.

Serves 4

Pheasant Fingers

Marinade   *Marinating time: overnight*

½ **cup olive oil**

¼ **cup white wine vinegar**

I clove garlic, crushed

I teaspoon dried fennel seed, crushed

I teaspoon chopped fresh parsley

I teaspoon chopped fresh oregano, or ½ **teaspoon dried**

2 whole pheasant breasts

I cup seasoned cracker meal

¾ **cup olive oil**

Combine the marinade ingredients. Remove the breast meat from the bone and cut into finger-sized pieces. Place the meat in a bowl, pour the marinade over, and marinate, covered, overnight in the refrigerator. Remove the pheasant but do not dry or drain it. Dredge the wet pieces in the cracker meal. Pat the meal firmly into the fowl on all sides. Discard the marinade, or freeze for future use.

Bring the oil to 325°F in an electric frying pan (see *Note*, page 80). Fry the pheasant fingers until golden. Drain on paper towels. Serve hot.

Serves 4 as an entrée; 6–8 as an appetizer

Harvest Soup

This is my family's traditional Thanksgiving Eve supper. I serve it with a green leafy salad and a loaf of homemade egg bread. The pumpkin tureen is dramatic and the soup delicious. Try making the soup several days in advance, as it becomes even more flavorful as it ages. Of course it's just as good served from a real tureen, but not as pretty.

1 pheasant

¼ cup plus ½ teaspoon salt

½ pound hot venison sausage, chopped

½ pound smoked sausage, chopped

½ cup chopped onion

2 quarts beef or chicken stock (see page 30)

4 medium potatoes, diced

1 (10-ounce) package frozen mixed vegetables

2 (16-ounce) cans creamed corn

1 can evaporated milk

3 bay leaves

1 teaspoon Old Bay Seafood Seasoning

1 teaspoon oregano

1 teaspoon black pepper

½ teaspoon paprika

1 medium-sized pumpkin to use as a tureen

Clean the pheasant and cut it into pieces. In a large stew pot, cover the pheasant pieces with 2 quarts of water and ¼ cup salt. Allow to soak for several hours. Drain, rinse, and pat dry.

Return the pheasant to the pot, cover with fresh water, and cook over medium heat for ½–¾ hour. Remove the meat and allow to cool. Pick the meat from the bones, cut into small pieces, and set aside. Add the sausages, onions, and stock to the pot, and bring to a boil. Lower the heat and simmer for 15 minutes. Add the potatoes and mixed vegetables, and boil 5 minutes longer. Add the chopped pheasant meat, corn, evaporated milk, bay leaves, seafood seasoning, oregano, pepper, paprika, and the remaining ½ teaspoon salt to the pot. Lower the heat to simmer and cook for 1 hour, to allow the flavors to blend. Stir frequently to prevent sticking.

Meanwhile, make the pumpkin tureen. Preheat the oven to 300°F. Wash the pumpkin and cut off the top as for a jack-o'-lantern. Scrape out the seeds from the cavity. Put the pumpkin on a baking sheet and bake for 20–30 minutes. The pumpkin should be warm, but not cooked through, as it must stay firm enough to use as a tureen.

When ready to serve, remove the bay leaves, bring the soup close to a boil, then ladle it into the pumpkin. Later, as you ladle the soup into individual bowls, scoop some softened, cooked pumpkin from the sides for garnish.

Serves 6–8

South Seas Fowl

2 pounds fowl (pheasant, doves, and/or quail)

Marinating time: 2–4 hours

I cup orange juice

4 tablespoons butter (½ stick), melted

4 tart apples (preferably Granny Smiths)

I lime

Clean the fowl and cut into serving-sized pieces. Whisk together the orange juice and melted butter. Pour over the fowl in a sealable plastic bag and marinate in the refrigerator for 2–4 hours, turning at least once. Preheat the oven to 300°F. Wash the apples and cut into slices. Slice the lime. Place the marinated fowl in a baking dish and cover with the marinade, sliced apples, and lime slices. Bake for 1–1½ hours, depending on the size of the pieces. The meat is done when the juices run clear.

Serves 4–6

Lemon Bourbon Fowl

The bourbon in this recipe permeates the fowl and imparts an excellent flavor. It has become a favorite summer picnic entrée, using chicken when game is not available.

2 or 3 lemons, depending on size

1 cup bourbon whiskey

3 or 4 pheasants, 3 quail, or 8 to 10 doves

Marinating time: 3–4 hours, plus overnight

Remove the zest from 1 lemon and set aside. Squeeze the lemon to make ½ cup of juice, supplementing with an additional lemon as necessary. Combine the lemon zest, lemon juice, and bourbon.

Clean and skin the fowl. Place meat-side down in a shallow baking dish and pour the lemon mixture over it. Marinate at room temperature for 3–4 hours, then refrigerate, covered, overnight. The next day, remove from the refrigerator and bring to room temperature before cooking.

Reserving the marinade, remove the fowl from the dish and arrange it on a broiler pan. Slice the remaining lemon as thinly as possible, top the fowl with the lemon slices, and baste with the lemon-bourbon marinade. Broil as far as possible from the heat, basting frequently with the marinade, until the juices run clear. This dish may also be cooked over charcoal or on a gas grill, basting frequently, over the lowest heat setting.

Serves 6–8

Waterfowl

As SOON AS any game is killed, the process of deterioration or decay begins. It is most important, therefore, to take the extra steps necessary to ensure that the birds you take home are in prime condition for the table. It is critical to disembowel and cool down the birds as soon as you can. Eviscerate the fowl in the field whenever possible, and during the warm fall days always hunt with an ice chest waiting to cool down the birds. Grass-eating ducks and geese are especially likely to lose their flavor if not cooled down, because the grasses they feed on ferment rapidly.

Waterfowl Servings
1 duck serves 2, depending on size.
1 goose serves 4–6, depending on size.

Removing Feathers
It is relatively easy to pluck the feathers from land fowl, but water-repellent birds, such as ducks and geese, present some difficulty. There are three recognized ways to remove feathers from waterfowl: (1) scald in hot water; (2) partially dry-pluck and dip in paraffin; and (3) dry-pluck, singe, and scrub. I describe these three methods below.

Scalding in Hot Water. Dipping waterfowl in plain hot water does not effectively remove the natural oils on the feathers; they will remain almost waterproof regardless of the temperature of the water. The addition of about 3 tablespoons of detergent per gallon of hot water cuts through that oil. Before scalding, remove the wings, head, and tail feathers. Immerse the fowl and work it up and down for about 45 seconds. Keep the bird submerged as much as possible (a wooden spoon is handy for this). Remove the bird and immediately plunge it into a cold-water bath to stop the scalding process. Using your fingers, rub off the feathers. If the feathers do not rub off easily, repeat the process. For geese, increase the submersion time in the hot water to about 90 seconds.

Partially Dry-Plucking and Dipping in Paraffin. You will need a bucket of paraffin for ducks, and a larger container for geese. The initial cost of the paraffin is high, but it can be used for a long time by straining out the feathers periodically. If you prefer, duck wax especially for this purpose is sold in sporting goods stores. Heating such a large quantity of wax can be dangerous, so be sure to have a stable work area. You will also need another container deep enough to cover the bird with cold water.

To dry-pluck waterfowl, lay the bird on its back in your left hand, grasping the bird over the wings and shoulders with the head away from you. Beginning at the base of its neck, take as many feathers in your right hand as you can and roll your hand outward with a quick, jerking motion. Remove all the feathers from a small spot before continuing. Work away from your body, up the bird's neck, until the upper part of the bird's body is bare. Then reverse the position of the fowl, placing the head and neck against your body, and continue plucking across the breast, by rolling your hand quickly. Repeat for the back. Dry-plucking is easiest right after a bird is killed.

When you have plucked as many feathers off the bird as possible, remove the tail feathers, wings, and head. Holding the feet, dip the partially cleaned bird in hot wax, then plunge it into cold water. Repeat this process until the bird is covered with a thick coat of wax. Then, using a knife, rip off the strips of wax. The remaining feathers and down will come off with the wax. This method takes some time to set up at first, but it really works well. Remove the feet and you have a neat, clean bird ready for the kitchen.

Dry-Plucking, Singeing, and Scrubbing. First pluck out as many feathers as possible, using the method described above. (No matter how hard you try, some fine down and feather filaments will be left on the bird.) When you have removed as many feathers as you can, pull out the tail feathers and cut off the head and wings. Hang the bird by the feet and singe off the remaining feathers. Uncle Bud uses the blue flame from a camp stove—we prefer a blowtorch. Both work well. Cleanup after singeing sometimes requires soap to remove the carbon from the skin. Wash and rinse the bird thoroughly and remove the feet before sending it to the kitchen.

River Ducks and Diving Ducks

There are three main types of ducks: river ducks, diving ducks, and domestic ducks. Organically grown domestic ducks are also now available and make excellent, elegant entrées. River and diving ducks are game birds and provide good hunting up and down the seacoasts of our country. In general, river ducks are the most palatable, but some species of diving ducks also make good eating.

River ducks feed in shallow water on insects, snails, frogs, and other aquatic life. This is the duck that simply "tips over" headfirst into the water to feed, as opposed to the diving duck, which disappears underwater for several minutes. Because of its diet, the wild river duck is prized for its meat.

The most popular of the river ducks is the mallard. All domestic ducks, except the Muscovy duck, are descended from the wild mallard. The mallard is an important game bird, as are the teal, pintail, black, gadwall, baldpate, shoveler, and wood ducks. Recipes in this section will specify which type of duck (river or diving) is appropriate for each recipe.

It is much more difficult to prepare a diving duck, such as a merganser, than a river duck. Diving ducks forage far below the surface of the water in search of their primary source of food—fish. Diving ducks are a culinary challenge and must be treated with care in the kitchen if we are to enjoy them, for their meat is understandably strong tasting. However, the excellent canvasback and ring-neck ducks are popular exceptions to this rule. If you have taken a diving duck, it is best to label it as such when storing it in the freezer.

Fish-eating fowl have rich dark meat that is almost always fishy tasting. There are several things that can be done to diminish and modify the strong flavor of these birds, however. Rubbing all surfaces of the bird with brandy, sherry, ginger, or lemon will help remove some of the strong flavor if this is done early enough before preparation for cooking. Refrigerate the treated bird for several hours before proceeding. Older birds will benefit from the application of meat tenderizer to all body surfaces, also several hours before cooking.

It is important to know as much as possible about your catch in order to prepare any kind of game, and this is especially true with duck.

As well as accounting for the type of fowl, successful cooking of all fowl depends on age, condition, and the care taken in the field. Birds should be cleaned or eviscerated immediately, and every attempt should be made to keep them cool. In general, young ducks will weigh less than 3 pounds, dressed. Older birds will weigh 3 to 6 pounds and have more fat per pound.

Many of the recipes in this section call for marinades and slow cooking, using citrus zest and liquors (bourbon, sherry, wine, vermouth, and tequila) to flavor, tenderize, and moisten the meat. Preparing diving duck, especially, is not something you can rush. Take the time to pretreat the fowl as described above; then allow the full marinating time called for (12–48 hours, depending on the recipe) and the full cooking time.

River Duck Salad

This salad is beautiful served in lettuce cups or on a wedge of fresh pineapple. It's an excellent way to use up leftover fowl.

6 duck breasts   *Marinating time: overnight*

2 cups water

1 (11-ounce) can mandarin oranges, drained

1 cup chopped celery

6 green onions, including tops, thinly sliced

1 cup chopped walnuts

1 cup Homemade French Dressing (see next page)

1 cup mayonnaise

Poach the duck breasts in 2 cups water in a covered pot until the meat pulls away from the bone, about 10 minutes. Remove the breasts from the pot and cool. Remove the meat from the bone and cut into bite-sized cubes. Add the oranges, celery, onions, and walnuts. Pour the dressing over the salad and toss to combine. Cover and refrigerate overnight. Drain off as much dressing as possible before serving, and mix in the mayonnaise.

Serves 8

Homemade French Dressing

*I avoid all prepared salad dressings. Several of my homemade
favorites—like this one—are scattered throughout the book.*

1 cup wine vinegar

1 cup vegetable oil

1 (8-ounce) can tomato sauce

1/2 cup water

3 tablespoons tomato paste

1 onion, chopped fine

1/2 cup sugar

4–5 cloves garlic, minced

2 teaspoons dry sherry

1 teaspoon pepper

1 teaspoon dry mustard

1/4 teaspoon celery seed

Combine all the ingredients in a blender and blend until smooth. Store
the extra dressing, bottled, in the refrigerator.

Yield: 3 1/2 cups

River Duck with Orange Glaze

1 duck
2 tablespoons butter
¼ cup brandy
3 carrots, chopped
2 sprigs fresh parsley
2 teaspoons thyme
2 bay leaves
1 cup pheasant or chicken stock (see page 68)
½ cup white wine
3 tablespoons orange zest, divided
3 oranges, sliced
½ cup orange marmalade

Preheat the oven to 375°F. Wash the duck and pat dry. Melt the butter in a Dutch oven and brown the duck all over. Pour the brandy over the duck, stand back, and light with a match. When the flames die down, add to the pan the carrots, parsley, thyme, bay leaves, stock, and wine. Sprinkle the duck with 2 tablespoons of the orange zest. Cover and bake for 1 hour, or until the meat juices run clear. Remove the duck to a warm serving platter. Strain the pan drippings and combine with the remaining 1 tablespoon zest and the sliced oranges. Bring to a boil on top of the stove and reduce for 5–6 minutes. Add the marmalade and stir to blend. Pour the sauce over the duck and serve immediately.

Serves 2

Grilled River Duck Breasts

I tablespoon butter, melted

Marinating time: 1 hour

2 teaspoons lemon juice

I teaspoon lemon zest

I teaspoon Worcestershire sauce

I teaspoon ketchup

½ teaspoon paprika

2 large duck breasts

Combine the melted butter, lemon juice, zest, Worcestershire sauce, and ketchup. Sprinkle the paprika on the duck breasts. Pour the sauce over the breasts and marinate, covered, at room temperature for 1 hour. Prepare a charcoal fire or preheat a gas grill. Reserving the marinade, remove the breasts and grill, 3 inches from the heat source, until brown (about 12 minutes). Baste frequently with the marinade. Cover the grill with a hood or foil and grill for 20 minutes more, lowering the heat if possible (when grilling over charcoal, raise the rack).

Note: You can use domestic duck in this recipe with equal success.

Serves 2–3

River Duck Creole

1 medium duck
2 tablespoons Kitchen Bouquet (see _Note_)
2 tablespoons light olive oil
1 medium onion, chopped
3 stalks celery, chopped
1 clove garlic, crushed
4 green onions, sliced
1 cup pheasant or chicken stock (see page 68)
1 chicken bouillon cube

Split the duck in half and brush all surfaces with Kitchen Bouquet. Allow to stand for 10 minutes. Using a pastry brush, coat all surfaces of the duck with the oil. In a heavy ovenproof skillet, brown the duck on all sides. Preheat the oven to 325°F. Remove the duck from the pan and add the chopped onion, celery, and garlic to the pan. Sauté until the celery and onions are tender. Return the duck to the pan and add the green onions, stock, and bouillon cube. Bake, covered, for 3 hours in the oven. Serve over rice.

Note: Kitchen Bouquet is a liquid seasoning, also called a gravy enhancer. It's available in most supermarkets.

Serves 2

Pot-Roasted River Ducks

This recipe makes a delicious gravy—serve it over rice.

4 stalks celery, sliced

1 bell pepper, chopped

3 cloves garlic, minced

1 medium onion, chopped

2 tart apples, quartered

2 ducks

3 tablespoons olive oil

½ cup chicken or pheasant stock (see page 68)

2 teaspoons cornstarch

½ cup cold water

Mix the celery, peppers, garlic, onions, and apples. Stuff the cavities of the ducks with this mixture and skewer the cavities closed. Heat the oil in a Dutch oven and brown the ducks in it. Cover tightly and braise over very low heat for 3–4 hours, or until the legs move freely and the meat is tender. Turn the ducks occasionally during cooking. Remove the ducks to a serving platter and add the stock to the pan. Mix the cornstarch with the water and stir until no lumps remain. Stir slowly into the stock and pan drippings at a slow boil until the broth thickens into gravy—about 2 minutes. Pour over the ducks and serve immediately.

Serves 4–6

Stewed River Duck

1 duck
8 tablespoons butter (1 stick)
2 onions, chopped (see Note)
3 teaspoons parsley
2 teaspoons basil
1 teaspoon oregano
1 teaspoon marjoram
1 teaspoon celery seed
1 teaspoon red pepper flakes
½ cup white rice

Place the duck in a large stewing pot and cover with water. Bring to a boil. Add the butter, onions, parsley, basil, oregano, marjoram, celery seed, and red pepper flakes. Simmer, covered, for 2 hours. Remove the duck to a serving platter and place in a warm (250°F) oven.

Add the rice to the stewing liquid in the pot, cover, and cook over low heat until most of the liquid has been absorbed, 15–20 minutes. Place the cooked rice around the duck and garnish with some celery and onion from the pot.

Note: To chop onions with ease, simply peel and, holding the onion upright, make ¼-inch-deep scores all across the top, being careful not to cut through. Turn the onion and make more cuts running perpendicular to the first, like a grid. Turn the onion on its side and slice as you would for rings. Instant chopped onion!

Serves 2

Sweet River Duck

4 ducks, quartered
½ cup apricot preserves
½ cup lemon juice
Zest of 1 lemon
1 lemon, sliced
½ teaspoon ginger

Marinating time: 6–8 hours
or overnight

Arrange the ducks in a baking dish and spread with the apricot preserves. Pour the lemon juice over the ducks. Sprinkle with the lemon zest. Cover and marinate in the refrigerator for at least 6–8 hours or overnight, turning several times. Preheat the oven to 350°F. Top the ducks with the lemon slices and sprinkle with the ginger. Bake for 1–1½ hours, or until the juices run clear.

Serves 6–8

Orange-Honey Merganser

1 or 2 mergansers
(diving ducks)

Marinating time: overnight

3 oranges

½ cup dark honey

½ cup bourbon

4 stalks celery, julienned

1 medium onion, sliced thin

2 cloves garlic, minced

Fresh parsley for garnish

Refer to the preparation of diving ducks on page 87.

Cut the duck(s) in half for better distribution of marinade flavors. Slice one orange and set aside. Remove the zest from the remaining two oranges, squeeze, and reserve the juice. Place the duck halves in a sealable plastic bag and cover with the orange zest and orange juice. Add the honey and bourbon to the bag. Seal, and marinate overnight in the refrigerator, turning occasionally. Do not skip or shorten this step.

Preheat the oven to 300°F. Reserving the marinade, remove the ducks from the bag and place them skin-side down in a baking dish. Into each cavity, layer the celery, onion, garlic, and orange slices. Bake for 30 minutes. Remove the ducks from the oven and pour the reserved marinade over them. Turn the ducks skin-side up, cover, and return to the oven. Bake for 45–50 minutes more, basting frequently. Remove the cover, increase the oven temperature to 450°F, and bake for 10 more minutes. Remove the ducks to a serving platter and garnish with parsley.

Serves 2

Sherried Diving Duck

2 ducks (merganser, canvasback, or ringneck)

3 cups milk

½ cup red sherry wine

1 cup flour

2 tablespoons butter

1 onion, chopped

1 green bell pepper, chopped

1 (10½-ounce) can cream of chicken soup (low fat if available)

½ cup white sherry wine

Marinating time: overnight plus 2–3 hours

Split the ducks in half. Place them in a sealable plastic bag with the milk. Refrigerate overnight, turning the bag at least once. Remove the ducks from the bag and discard the milk. Pat the ducks dry. Place the ducks in a baking dish and pour the red sherry over them. Marinate at room temperature for 2–3 hours. Preheat the oven to 250°F.

Remove the ducks from the sherry and dredge them in the flour. Melt the butter in a skillet and brown the ducks until just golden. Remove the ducks from the skillet and place them in a baking dish. In the same skillet, sauté the onions and green peppers in the remaining butter. Add the soup and the white sherry and mix well. Pour over the ducks. Cover and bake for 60 minutes.

Serves 4

Lemon Baked Diving Duck

Low fat

8 diving ducks, halved
1 lemon
2 onions
2 cups lemon juice
½ cup gin
1 clove garlic, chopped
2 teaspoons oregano
1 teaspoon coarsely ground pepper
3 tablespoons lemon zest
Salt, to taste

Marinating time: 4–6 hours

Place the ducks flesh-side down in a baking dish or in sealable plastic bags. Slice the lemon and 1 onion and cover the ducks with the slices. Chop the second onion, then process in the blender with the lemon juice. Add the gin and garlic, process until well blended, and pour over the ducks. Sprinkle with the oregano, pepper, lemon zest, and salt. Marinate in the refrigerator, covered, for 4–6 hours.

Preheat the oven to 250°F. Place the ducks in a large roasting pan with the marinade and bake for 2 hours, basting frequently. Uncover and bake at 350°F for 15 minutes more, or until the juices run clear and the legs move freely.

Serves 6–8

Sweet Red Diving Duck

Low fat

2 ducks, quartered   *Marinating time: overnight*
1 cup port
3 tablespoons Worcestershire sauce
½ cup red currant jelly
3 tablespoons butter

Place the duck pieces in a baking dish. Combine the port, Worcestershire sauce, and jelly, and pour over the ducks. Marinate, covered, in the refrigerator overnight.

Preheat the oven to 250°F. Cover the ducks and bake in the marinade for 40 minutes. Remove the cover, turn the duck pieces, and dot with the butter. Return the dish to the oven and bake, uncovered, for 20 minutes more. Turn off the oven and allow the dish to stand another 20 minutes without opening the door. Remove from the oven and serve immediately.

Serves 4

Japanese Diving Ducks

Low fat

Marinade   *Marinating time: 48 hours or more*
1 cup tamari or soy sauce
½ cup dry vermouth
¼ cup olive oil
2 cloves garlic, minced
1 teaspoon orange zest
1 ½ teaspoons grated gingerroot

4 ducks, halved

Combine all the marinade ingredients. Place the halved ducks meat-side down in a baking dish, pour the marinade over them, and cover. Marinate in the refrigerator for at least 48 hours, turning frequently. Place the ducks, still in the marinade, in a cold oven. Turn the temperature to 300°F and bake for 35 minutes. Turn the duck halves and bake for another 20 minutes. Remove the ducks from the marinade and broil 4 inches from the heat for 5–6 minutes, or until the skin is crispy and the juices run clear.

Serves 4

Oranged Diving Duck

Low fat

2 ducks, split
5 oranges
2 onions, thinly sliced
2 teaspoons cornstarch
1 cup cold pheasant or chicken stock (see page 68)
¼ cup red currant jelly

Preheat the oven to 375°F. Place split ducks skin-side down in a baking pan. Slice two of the oranges. Fill each duck cavity with alternating slices of onion and orange. Bake for 1 hour.

While the ducks are baking, remove the zest from the remaining three oranges; reserve. Slice one of the oranges and set aside for garnish. Squeeze the two remaining oranges and reserve the juice. Dissolve the cornstarch in the cold stock, and add the orange juice. Heat and stir. Add the currant jelly and set aside.

Remove the ducks from the oven and turn them skin-side up. Reduce the oven temperature to 250°F. Sprinkle the orange zest evenly over the ducks, return them to the oven, and bake for 1½–2 hours more, or until the juices run clear. Remove the ducks from the baking pan and keep warm. Pour off all but 2 tablespoons of drippings from the baking dish. Put the baking pan on the stove top over medium heat and add the stock mixture to the pan. Simmer briskly, whisking the mixture, until the pan juices are incorporated and the mixture has thickened into gravy. Arrange the ducks on a serving platter, pour the gravy over, and garnish with the reserved orange slices.

Serves 2 generously

Diving Duck Tequila

Low fat

8 ducks, halved

**2 large onions, pureed
in a food processor or blender**

2½ cups orange juice

I cup tequila

3 tablespoons orange zest

2 cloves garlic, minced

2 teaspoons oregano

2 teaspoons cumin

I teaspoon coarsely ground black pepper

*Marinating time: 4–6 hours plus
overnight, plus 3–4 hours*

Place the ducks in sealable plastic bags. To make the marinade, combine the onion puree, orange juice, tequila, orange zest, garlic, oregano, cumin, and pepper. Pour the marinade over the ducks, dividing equally among the bags. Marinate for 4–6 hours at room temperature, then refrigerate overnight.

Remove the ducks from the refrigerator 3–4 hours before baking. Continue to marinate at room temperature, turning the bags frequently. Place the ducks with the marinade in a large covered roasting pan in a cold oven. Turn the oven to 350°F and bake for 1 hour. Reduce the heat to 250°F and bake for 45–60 minutes more. Baste frequently and keep the dish tightly covered. If desired, remove the lid during the last 15 minutes to brown the meat. The ducks are done when the legs move freely and the juices run clear.

Serves 6–8 hungry people

Stuffed Duck with Spicy Fruit Dressing

Stuffing
3 cups toasted bread cubes
3 cups diced apple
½ cup cubed orange sections
3 tablespoons chopped onion
Zest and juice of 1 orange
1 teaspoon lemon zest
1 teaspoon grated gingerroot
1 teaspoon salt
¼ teaspoon ground cloves
Pepper, to taste

2 small ducks

Preheat the oven to 350°F. Combine the bread cubes, apples, orange sections, onions, orange and lemon zests, gingerroot, salt, cloves, and pepper. (Reserve the orange juice for basting the ducks.) Put the stuffing mixture into the body cavities of the cleaned ducks; fill loosely and do not pack. (This amount is enough for two small ducks or one 4-pound duck.) Roast the ducks for 2 hours, basting with the reserved orange juice. Increase the heat to 425°F and roast for 20 minutes longer, or until the legs move easily.

Note: After serving the ducks, remove the stuffing from the cavities and refrigerate any leftover meat. Never store any fowl with stuffing in the body cavity; this is conducive to bacteria growth.

Serves 2–4

Martini Baked Duck

This dish is best prepared the day before serving, allowing the flavors to blend and the cook to rest.

Marinade   *Marinating time: overnight*

1 quart dry white vermouth

2 cups water

1 onion, pureed
   in a food processor or blender

3 tablespoons safflower oil

2 jiggers gin

2 teaspoons ground pepper

1 teaspoon melted butter

1 dash hot pepper sauce

8 ducks, cleaned, halved, and skinned

8 bay leaves, cut in half

2 large onions, cut in eighths

1 navel orange, chopped, with juice

½ cup chopped fresh parsley

Preheat the oven to 275°F. In a large Dutch oven, combine the marinade ingredients. Set aside half the mixture. Heat the remaining marinade to a simmer, then place the duck halves flesh-side down in the pan. Top each duck half with a bay leaf, an onion section, and some chopped orange, orange juice, and parsley. Bake for 3½ hours, basting occasionally. Remove from the oven. Pour the reserved marinade over the ducks, cover, and let stand in the refrigerator for 1–2 hours, or overnight if desired. To serve, cover and bake at 350°F for ½ hour, or until heated through. Garnish with orange and parsley, if desired.

Serves 6–8

Chinese Sauced Goose Breasts

After attending an eight-course Chinese New Year's feast, I came home enamored of this sauce, used on pork ribs. After trial, error, research, and personalization, this recipe emerged. This is also an exceptional way to prepare beef or pork ribs. It is still my son Scott's favorite rib dinner, which we make from his own steers.

I cup water

4 to 6 chunks Chinese rock sugar
   or yellow lump sugar (see *Note*)

I ounce dried star anise (see *Note*)

¼ cup soy sauce

¼ cup dry sherry

I whole goose breast

Marinating time: 48 hours

Bring the water to a boil in a saucepan and add the sugar, star anise, and soy sauce. Lower the heat and simmer until the sugar dissolves. Remove from the heat, add the sherry, and allow to cool.

Bone and cube the goose breast. Pour the cooled sauce over the meat and marinate in the refrigerator, covered, for at least 48 hours.

Preheat the oven to 275°F. Place the goose with the sauce in a baking dish, cover, and bake for 1–1½ hours. Remove the cover for the last 15 minutes of baking time.

Note: Chinese rock sugar and star anise are available in Chinese markets and health food stores. I do sometimes substitute brown sugar if I'm out of lump sugar, but I always have bags of star anise in the freezer.

Save the leftover sauce to use over and over. It ripens and increases in flavor each time. Strain, skim, and freeze—then add to the new sauce for each preparation.

Serves 4

Roast Goose

This preparation tastes remarkably like beef and yields a very rich, all-dark-meat entrée.

1 goose   *Marinating time: overnight*

2 cups sweet red vermouth

1 onion, quartered

3 ribs celery with leaves, roughly chopped

2 tart apples, quartered

Flavored meat tenderizer, optional (see Note)

Place the goose in a deep container and pour the vermouth over it. Turn to coat the entire bird. Cover the dish tightly with plastic wrap and marinate overnight in the refrigerator, turning at least four times. Preheat the oven to 250°F. Reserving the marinade, remove the goose from the dish. Place the onions, celery, and apples in the body cavity. Place the goose on a roasting rack in an open pan. Roast for ½ hour per pound, basting frequently with the reserved marinade.

Note: The feeding ground of waterfowl determines the taste of its flesh. If your goose has lived on fish and water animals, it will taste strong and fishy. If it fed on corn and meal, its meat will be delicious and mild. So vary your marinating time to compensate for the diet of your goose. If you fear your goose will be too strong, fishy, or tough, sprinkle the body cavity generously with tenderizer and allow to stand another hour before roasting.

Yield: ½ pound of goose per serving

Roast Wild Turkey

A 20- to 22-pound domestic turkey is magnificent prepared in this manner, should your hunter not come through with a wild bird.

I wild turkey
4 tablespoons butter (½ stick), plus more for basting
I large onion, diced
½ cup chopped celery
I pound chorizo or linguiça sausage (see *Note*)
I (16-ounce) package bread stuffing, or 6 cups cubed bread
3 eggs, lightly beaten

Brine the turkey in a strong solution of salted water for 1 hour. Rinse and dry thoroughly. Preheat the oven to 325°F. Melt 4 tablespoons butter in a large pot and sauté the onions and celery until soft, stirring frequently. Remove from the heat. Add the crumbled or chopped sausage, along with the bread cubes and beaten eggs. Mix well. Add ¼ cup of hot water to moisten. The stuffing is moist enough when a handful forms a ball. Add more water if necessary.

Carefully loosen the skin from the turkey breast by moving your fingers slowly back and forth underneath the skin, being careful not to tear it, until the entire breast skin is loose. Insert the stuffing between the skin and the breast, covering the entire breast area. This should use all the filling, as the skin will stretch. This method of stuffing will hold the juices in the meat, making it moist and flavorful. (Stuffing by this method also reduces the cooking time, as the heat does not have to penetrate all the way into the bird to cook the stuffing.) Cover the bird with a piece of soft muslin or cheesecloth that has been dampened, then saturated with melted butter. Place the bird in the oven, legs to the rear, for even cooking. Roast in the preheated oven, basting with melted butter, for 3 to 4 hours, or 40 minutes per pound.

Note: Chorizo is a spicy Mexican pork sausage, and linguiça is a slender, garlic-flavored Portuguese sausage. Remove the casing and crumble or chop the sausage before cooking.

Yield: A wild turkey serves 4–6; a domestic turkey 10–12

Wild Turkey Breast Tequila

1 wild turkey breast, cut in half	*Marinating time: 2–3 hours*
1 large onion, sliced	
1 cup lime juice	
½ cup tequila	
½ cup water	
1 clove garlic, minced	
2 teaspoons oregano	
2 teaspoons dried basil, or 6 fresh leaves	
1 teaspoon coarsely ground pepper	
Salt to taste	

Place the turkey breast flesh-side down in a baking dish. Cover with onion slices. Combine the remaining ingredients in a blender and blend until smooth. Pour the mixture over the breasts and marinate, covered, at room temperature for 2–3 hours. Preheat the oven to 350°F.

Roast the turkey with the marinade, covered, for 1 hour. Baste several times with the pan juices during cooking. Reduce the oven temperature to 250°F and cook for 30–40 minutes more. Just before serving, turn the breasts skin-side up and run under the broiler for 3–4 minutes to brown.

Note: To make turkey stock for later use, place the remaining parts of your turkey (the carcass—bones, wings, legs, neck, and back) in a large pot with water to cover. After the pot comes to a boil, lower the heat and add onion, celery, and oregano to taste. Gently simmer for 1 hour. Strain and reserve the stock for use in gravies, soups, and sauces. Pick the meat from the bones and add to the stock to make soup. Freeze the stock in ice cube trays, then store the homemade bouillon cubes in sealable plastic freezer bags. Use 2–4 cubes in place of 1 commercial bouillon cube, or ½ teaspoon of powdered bouillon.

Serves 4–6

New England Wild Turkey

I prepare small domestic turkeys this way and cook them on a gas grill with a rotisserie. The bacon bastes the breast as the turkey cooks, imparting a subtle smoky flavor to the meat. Try this with chicken, too.

1 wild turkey
½ pound bacon, thickly sliced
3 tablespoons softened butter or margarine

Wash and dress the turkey. Preheat the oven to 350°F. Carefully loosen the skin from the breast by moving your fingers slowly back and forth underneath the skin, being careful not to tear it, until the entire breast skin is loose. Place the bacon slices on the breast, under the skin. Sew or skewer the skin and legs together, and brush the breast skin with the softened butter or margarine. Roast until the leg or wing moves freely, about 40 minutes per pound.

Note: If you are watching your calories and fat, substitute turkey bacon or lean Canadian bacon.

Serves 6–8

Roasted Breast of Old Tom Turkey

This is a good recipe for older birds. The slow simmer in vermouth will make anything tender. Use the remaining turkey parts for soup or stock (see Note, *page 108).*

1 whole wild turkey breast   *Marinating time: overnight*
1 large onion, sliced
2 cups sweet red vermouth
Dash of paprika

Cut the turkey breast in half and place skin-side down in a roasting pan or covered casserole dish. Scatter the sliced onion on top of the breasts and cover with the vermouth. Marinate overnight, covered, in the refrigerator. Bring the turkey to room temperature before roasting. Preheat the oven to 250°F. Roast the breasts in a covered pan for 2 hours. Remove the lid and turn the breasts skin-side up. Sprinkle with the paprika, increase the oven temperature to 350°F, and roast, uncovered, until tender. Depending on the size of the breasts, this should take ½–¾ hour more.

Serves 4–6

Spring Turkey with Cattails

Wild turkey and cattails! What a conversation starter. This is not only good, it's exciting as well, especially if you take the time to gather the tender young cattail shoots yourself. (See page 193 for a list of field guides to wild edibles.) I like to think of recipes like these as grounding, *especially for youngsters! They tie us to the land and to our heritage.*

4 tablespoons butter (½ stick)
5 tablespoons flour
1 (12-ounce) can evaporated milk
½ cup sliced green onions
2 cups pheasant or chicken stock (see page 68)
1⅓ cups Minute rice, uncooked
1½ cups cooked young cattails (or asparagus)
2 cups cooked and diced wild turkey
1½ cups grated cheddar cheese
3 tablespoons slivered almonds

Preheat the oven to 375°F. Melt the butter in a saucepan and stir in the flour to make a paste. Add the evaporated milk and stir over medium heat until smooth and thick. Add the onions and simmer 3–4 minutes. Add the stock and stir to heat through. Pour the rice into a greased 2-quart baking dish, then pour the sauce over the rice. Top with the cattail shoots and the diced turkey. Sprinkle with the cheese. Bake for 30 minutes, or until warmed through and bubbling. Top with the slivered almonds and run under the broiler until the almonds are golden and the cheese is bubbly.

Note: This dish can be made ahead and baked later, or made ahead, baked, refrigerated or frozen, and reheated. This is a great way to get rid of any leftover fowl.

Serves 6

Ham and Wild Turkey Soup

This soup was developed after the winter holidays, when we all have leftover ham and turkey. The addition of a ham hock makes the broth more flavorful. The meat of the ham hock is one of my family's favorites, thanks to my daughter Karen. She subsisted on chicken and ham hocks during her college years, and really introduced them to us.

1 ham hock
1 teaspoon light olive oil
1 cup diced celery
1 medium onion, diced
1 cup thinly sliced carrots
2 cups pheasant or chicken stock (see page 68)
1 cup cubed cooked ham
1 to 2 cups cubed cooked wild turkey
1 (28-ounce) can tomatoes, chopped, with juice
1 cup acini di pepe (or any other small pasta)
1 teaspoon basil
1 teaspoon thyme
½ teaspoon oregano
½ teaspoon black pepper
Grated Parmesan cheese

In a large pot, cover the ham hock with water and simmer slowly for 4–5 hours, or until the meat is tender and flakes away from the bone. Cool and reserve the broth. When the ham hock is cool enough to handle, remove the meat from the bone, cut into small pieces, and set aside. Discard the fat. When the broth has cooled, skim to remove the fat. In a large soup pot, heat the oil and sauté the celery, onions, and carrots. Add the stock and the reserved ham broth and bring to a boil. Lower the heat and simmer for 15–20 minutes. Add the cubed ham, reserved ham hock meat, and turkey; stir to combine. Add the tomatoes with their juice, and the pasta, basil, thyme, oregano, and pepper. Simmer for 1 hour over low heat. Serve with a garnish of Parmesan cheese floated in each bowl.

Serves 4–6

Wild Fowl Supreme

This is also an excellent preparation for organic or farm-raised fowl.

⅔ **cup long-grain brown rice**

3 tablespoons butter

3 cups wild fowl meat, cooked, deboned, and cut into chunks (pheasant, turkey, goose, duck, quail, or a mixture of leftovers)

½ **cup slivered almonds**

I sweet red bell pepper, sliced

I½ **cups sliced mushrooms**

3 tablespoons cornstarch

I¼ **cups pheasant or chicken stock (see page 68)**

I cup cream or evaporated milk

I teaspoon Bell's Poultry Seasoning

¼ **teaspoon basil**

¼ **teaspoon oregano**

Salt and pepper, to taste

Cook the rice according to package directions. Generously butter a baking dish with 1 tablespoon of the butter. Arrange the fowl pieces over the bottom of the dish. Cover with the cooked rice and sprinkle with the almonds. Top with the red peppers and mushrooms. Melt the remaining 2 tablespoons of butter and add the cornstarch, stirring constantly to form a paste. Add the stock and cream or milk and stir until a smooth, thick sauce forms. Add the poultry seasoning, basil, oregano, salt, and pepper and simmer for 3–4 minutes more. Preheat the oven to 350°F. Pour the sauce over the casserole, cover, and bake for 45 minutes, or until heated through and bubbling.

Note: This casserole can be assembled and frozen before baking. If you do this, allow the casserole to thaw before cooking.

Serves 4

Squab à la Crapaudine

Squab are young pigeons, but squab sounds so much more palatable than pigeon to most of us. Squab are usually expensive, as they are considered a great delicacy. They should be served well done. Allow 1 or 2 squab per serving, and expect them to be eaten with the fingers—the birds are too small to get all the meat off the tiny bones with a knife and fork.

1 or 2 squab per serving
Melted butter

Split each squab down the center of the breast and flatten with a rolling pin. Place in a roasting pan and broil under medium heat, turning each bird several times and brushing well with melted butter. The squab is done when very tender, and browned on the outside. Season to taste.

Roast Stuffed Squab

Stuffing
6 tablespoons butter (¾ stick)
½ cup dry white wine
1 onion, minced
1 cup fine bread crumbs
1 cup browned ground sausage
¼ cup chopped fresh parsley

4 to 8 squab

Preheat the oven to 325°F. In a saucepan, melt the butter with the white wine. Reserve half the mixture. In the remaining wine-butter mixture in the saucepan, cook the onion until translucent. Remove from the heat and stir in the bread crumbs, sausage, and parsley. Stuff each bird loosely with this mixture. Arrange the birds in a baking pan and cover with foil. Roast for ½ hour. Then begin to baste with the reserved butter-and-wine mixture at 15-minute intervals, until the juices run clear, about 1 more hour.

Serves 2–4

Baked Squab

Baked squab may be chilled and served cold as a picnic entrée.

½ **cup safflower oil**
¼ **cup dry white wine**
4 squab
4 tablespoons butter (½ stick), melted

Marinating time: 2–3 hours

In a covered dish or sealable plastic bag, marinate the squab in the oil and wine for 2–3 hours. Preheat the oven to 325°F. Remove the squab from the marinade, brush with half of the melted butter, and roast, basting frequently with the remaining butter.

Serves 2

Scott's Ruffed Grouse

The elusive ruffed grouse has a large, meaty breast and is very tender. The meat is predominantly white and the flavor mild.

Credit for this recipe goes to my son Scott, an avid and accomplished outdoorsman. He taught me much about the preparation of wild game, but most of all he motivated me to keep trying and cheered my culinary successes.

This master recipe makes one serving; of course you can multiply it by as many grouse as you have available.

1 quart water	*Marinating time: 24 hours*
½ cup salt	
1 grouse, cleaned and skinned	
2 large onions	
1 large apple	
3 slices bacon	

Combine the water and salt to make a solution and soak the grouse in it for several hours. Rinse clean to remove the salt and any blood. Chop 1 onion coarsely and stuff into the cavity of the bird. Wrap the grouse tightly in plastic wrap, or place in a sealable plastic bag, squeezing out all the air. Refrigerate overnight.

The next day, remove the chopped onion from the cavity and discard. Preheat the oven to 300°F. Chop the second onion and dice the apple, and place them in the cavity. Drape the bacon slices over the breast; cover the bird with foil, or put it in a baking pan with a lid. Bake for 1 hour (longer if you are roasting several birds). Test for doneness by moving the leg bone. It should move freely in its socket.

Serves 1

Quail with Wild Rice and Sherry Sauce

Try this excellent recipe with pheasant, dove, or woodcock, or any organic domestic fowl.

8 tablespoons butter (1 stick), divided
8 green onions and tops, sliced thin
1 cup sliced mushrooms
1¾ cups pheasant or chicken stock (see page 68)
½ cup sherry
¼ cup chopped fresh parsley
1 teaspoon sage
¼ teaspoon pepper
2 chicken livers
2 chicken necks
1 cup wild rice
8 quail
Watercress for garnish
Sherry Sauce (see next page)

Melt 4 tablespoons of the butter in a skillet and sauté the onions and mushrooms for 5 minutes. Set aside. In a saucepan, combine the pheasant or chicken stock, sherry, parsley, sage, pepper, livers, and necks. Bring to a boil, then add the wild rice. Lower the heat, cover the pan, and cook gently for about 45 minutes, or until the liquid has been absorbed and the rice is tender.

Preheat the oven to 325°F. Discard the chicken necks. Chop the chicken livers finely and return to the rice mixture. Add the mushrooms and onions to the rice and stir gently to combine. Use the rice mixture to stuff the quail. Place the stuffed birds in a shallow baking pan and roast for 1½ hours. Melt the remaining 4 tablespoons of butter and use to baste the quail three or four times during baking. Garnish with watercress and serve with Sherry Sauce.

Serves 6–8

Sherry Sauce

4 tablespoons butter (½ stick)
¼ cup flour
2 teaspoons paprika
¾ cup light sherry
¾ cup pheasant or chicken stock (see page 68)
I cup sour cream
Dash garlic powder, to taste

Melt the butter in a saucepan, then blend in the flour and paprika. Stir to form a smooth paste or roux, and heat gently until bubbling. Combine the sherry and the stock. Add slowly to the roux, stirring briskly to incorporate. Cook over medium heat until thickened and smooth. Gently blend in the sour cream, add the garlic powder, and heat through.

Poached Doves in Peach Broth

One year, the peach tree my son Scott had planted long ago on our front lawn put on a prolific display of the most beautiful, sweet fruit we'd eaten in a long time. We consumed fresh peaches for breakfast, for desserts, and in jams, and our little tree was still producing. In looking for new ways to enjoy this fruit, we came up with this dish.

8 doves

8 ripe peaches

4 tablespoons butter (½ stick), melted

8 slices French bread

Additional butter for the bread

Preheat the oven to 275°F. Place the doves in a deep baking dish. Peel the peaches, cut into rough pieces, and puree in a blender. Add the melted butter and blend. Pour the peach-butter mixture over the doves and cover. Bake for 45–50 minutes, or until the juices run clear and the legs move freely. Remove the doves from the pan, reserving the peach broth.

Toast the bread lightly and butter it generously. Just before serving, run the bread under the broiler until the butter sizzles. Place 1 dove on top of each bread slice, and pass the peach broth at the table.

Serves 8

Dove-Peach Casserole

1 tablespoon butter
1 tablespoon vegetable oil
8 doves
1 large onion, sliced
6 to 8 large ripe peaches
3 tablespoons white wine vinegar
1 tablespoon soy sauce
1 tablespoon cornstarch
1 tablespoon orange marmalade

Preheat the oven to 375°F. Heat the butter and oil in a skillet. Brown the doves gently on all sides just until golden. Cover, reduce the heat, and cook for 6–8 minutes. Remove the doves from the skillet and arrange in a baking dish. In the remaining fat in the skillet, sauté the onions until translucent. Peel the peaches and mash into a paste or puree a blender. Mix the vinegar, soy sauce, and cornstarch to make a smooth paste. Add the marmalade and peach puree. Pour into the skillet and stir until boiling. Reduce the heat and simmer for 5 minutes. Pour the peach mixture over the doves and cover the baking dish. Bake for 15–20 minutes, or until the legs move freely and the juices run clear. Remove the lid, turn off the oven, and allow to stand in the oven for 10 more minutes before serving.

Serves 4

Dove Gumbo

Serve this wonderful gumbo over rice. It can be made with any organic domestic fowl, cut into serving-size pieces

4 tablespoons vegetable oil

4 to 6 doves, split in half

I large onion, chopped

6 cups pheasant or chicken stock, heated (see page 68)

4 to 6 green onions, sliced, including tops

3 tablespoons chopped fresh parsley

2 tablespoons dried thyme, or 3 sprigs fresh

¼ teaspoon pepper

I pound smoked venison sausage or andouille sausage

I (10-ounce) package frozen okra

I pint shucked raw oysters

I tablespoon filé powder (see Note)

I clove garlic, minced

In a heavy pot, heat the oil and brown the doves. Remove the doves and sauté the onions in the remaining oil just until soft. Return the doves to the pot, cover with the stock, and add the green onions, parsley, thyme, and pepper. Cook over low heat until the doves are tender, 30–45 minutes. Cut the sausage into 1-inch slices and add to the pot with the okra. Cook for 15 minutes over medium heat. Add the oysters and their liquid and cook 6 minutes more. Skim off the excess fat. Remove from the heat and add the filé powder and garlic, stirring well to combine.

Note: Filé is the ground leaf of the sassafras plant, and is available in most gourmet shops. Add filé powder only after the gumbo is removed from the heat. It will thicken the stew too much if heated.

Serves 4–6

Limed Doves

1 cup light oil

Marinating time: overnight

1 cup fresh lime juice

Zest of 2 limes

3 cloves garlic, minced

3 stems cilantro, rinsed and chopped

½ teaspoon pepper

6 to 8 doves, split in half

Mix the oil, lime juice, lime zest, garlic, cilantro, and pepper. Shake or beat to combine well. Place the cleaned and split doves in a sealable plastic bag and pour the marinade over them. Refrigerate overnight, or up to 24 hours. Roast over coals or on a grill for about 45 minutes, turning and basting frequently. The birds are cooked when the legs move freely and the juices run clear.

Serves 4

Hassenpfeffer

*My family sold domestic rabbit in our meat market in the 1950s.
It was very popular and widely available.*

I rabbit, cut into
   serving-size pieces

4 cups wine vinegar

I tablespoon salt

I tablespoon pickling spices

I tablespoon peppercorns

2 bay leaves

I cup chopped onions, divided

2 tablespoons cooking oil

2 tablespoons flour

I cup cold water

I teaspoon cinnamon

½ teaspoon allspice

Marinating time: 24 hours

Place the rabbit pieces in a bowl or plastic bag and cover with the vinegar. Add the salt, pickling spices, peppercorns, bay leaves, and ½ cup of the onions. Marinate in the refrigerator for 24 hours. Remove the rabbit from the marinade and place in a large pot. Cover with boiling water and simmer for about 1½ hours, or until the rabbit is tender. Strain and reserve the broth. Remove the meat from the bones and set aside. Heat the oil in a frying pan and blend in the flour, stirring constantly to make a roux. Add 1 cup cold water and whisk until smooth. Cook until thickened. Add the rabbit, 2 cups of the strained broth, and the cinnamon, allspice, and remaining ½ cup onions, and simmer for 1 more hour. Remove the bay leaves before serving. Serve over noodles.

Serves 2–4

Rabbit Burgundy

1 ½ cups hearty Burgundy

Marinating time: 2–3 hours

3 green onions, sliced

3 cloves garlic, minced

½ teaspoon basil

½ teaspoon thyme

5 peppercorns, crushed

2 rabbits, cut into serving-size pieces

4 tablespoons oil

Combine the wine, green onions, garlic, basil, thyme, and peppercorns in a bowl or plastic bag. Add the rabbit and marinate for 2–3 hours in the refrigerator, stirring or turning several times. Remove the rabbit from the marinade, reserving the marinade, and pat dry.

Preheat the oven to 300°F. Heat the oil in a skillet. Add the rabbit and sauté until golden, but do not overcook. Drain the rabbit and place it in a baking dish. Pour the marinade over and bake, covered, for 1 hour.

Serves 4–6

Rabbit Stew

No fat

**2 cups dried lima beans, soaked overnight
   in 1½ quarts water**
**1 small rabbit, cut into
   serving-size pieces**
5 medium carrots, sliced
2 green bell peppers, chopped
1 medium onion, diced
1 clove garlic
2 bay leaves
2 teaspoons salt
¼ teaspoon pepper

Drain and rinse the soaked beans. Place the rabbit in a pot with the drained beans and add 1¼ quarts of fresh water to cover. Add the carrots, peppers, onions, garlic, bay leaves, and salt and pepper. Simmer for 1 hour, adding more water if needed, until the rabbit is tender. Remove the bay leaves before serving.

Serves 4

Squirrel Casserole

My friend Alice used this recipe to prepare her new stepson Trevor's squirrels. He was duly impressed!

3 or 4 squirrels, cleaned
1½ cups chopped onions
1 cup sliced mushrooms
6 cups cooked rice
1 teaspoon salt
1 clove garlic, crushed
½ teaspoon oregano
2 tablespoons cornstarch
½ cup water
1 cup grated Muenster cheese

In a large pot, cover the squirrels with water and cook, covered, until tender, about 1 hour. Reserve the broth. Remove the squirrels and allow them to cool before taking the meat off the bones. Preheat the oven to 350°F. Cut the meat into bite-sized pieces. Add the onions and mushrooms to the meat. Put the rice into a greased casserole. Top with the meat mixture and sprinkle with the salt, garlic, and oregano. Combine the cornstarch and the water; whisk into the reserved broth and simmer until thick, 2–3 minutes. Pour the gravy over the casserole. Bake until heated through, about 45 minutes. Top with the cheese, and run under the broiler to brown.

Serves 4

Squirrel à l'Orange

L. James Bashline was an associate editor for Field and Stream *magazine. An outdoors enthusiast, author of several books, and a fine hand in the kitchen, Jim claims this is his favorite squirrel recipe.*

2 squirrels, cleaned
I egg
I cup evaporated milk
½ cup orange juice, divided
½ cup flour
2 to 4 tablespoons port
½ cup oil

Cut each squirrel into six pieces—four legs and two back pieces. Parboil in salted water for 40 minutes. Drain the squirrel pieces and pat dry. Beat the egg and whisk it into the evaporated milk. Slowly whisk in ¼ cup of the orange juice. Dip the squirrel pieces into this mixture, then roll them in the flour. Heat the oil in a large skillet and fry the squirrel pieces over medium heat until golden. Drizzle the remaining ¼ cup orange juice and the port over the nearly cooked pieces. Pieces are done when they can be easily pierced with a toothpick.

Serves 4

Joe Cahn's Jambalaya

*While visiting New Orleans, I was fortunate enough to meet
the owner and driving force behind the New Orleans School of
Cooking, Joseph Cahn. Joe is a true disciple of Louisiana cuisine
and a native son his city can be proud of. After attending his
school, I couldn't wait to get home and improvise (as Joe
encourages you to do) with pheasant and venison sausage and
rabbit. Here are the resulting recipes—a taste of Louisiana à la
wild game.*

I rabbit

¼ cup vegetable shortening

1½ pounds venison sausage, cut into bite-sized pieces
(see page 41)

4 cups diced onions

2 cups diced celery

2 cups chopped green bell pepper

I garlic toe, chopped (see *Note*)

I teaspoon paprika

5 cups pheasant or chicken stock (see page 68)

3 heaping teaspoons salt

Cayenne pepper, to taste

4 cups long-grain white rice

I cup chopped green onions

I cup chopped fresh parsley

Place the rabbit in a large pot and add 7 cups of water. Bring to a boil,
then reduce the heat to a simmer and cook for ½ hour. Remove the rabbit
to cool, reserving the liquid for stock. When the rabbit is cool enough to
handle, remove the meat from the bones and cut into bite-sized pieces.

Place the vegetable shortening in a heavy pot and heat until melted.
Add the sausage and sauté for 10–15 minutes, stirring frequently, until
cooked and browned. Remove from the pot. Add the onions, celery, and
green peppers to the oil and sauté until the vegetables are tender, about
10 minutes. Remove from the heat. Add the sausage, rabbit, garlic, and
paprika, stirring well after each addition. Pour the stock into the pot and
return to the heat. Bring to a boil. Add the salt, cayenne, and rice. Stir to

combine and return to a boil. Cover and reduce the heat to a simmer. Cook for 30–35 minutes without peeking. After 30 minutes, peek, stir, and test the rice for doneness. Add the green onions and parsley, stir, and serve.

Note: In Creole cooking, one clove of garlic is referred to as a toe. Sometimes you'll see this ingredient listed as simply "1 toe"!

Serves 6

Joe Cahn's New Orleans Gumbo

The secret to Joe's gumbo is the roux. He uses lard, I use vegetable shortening. Whatever you use, Joe advises, keep the fat hot and the whisk moving, and it will come out perfect every time.

½ cup vegetable shortening

1 pheasant, cut into serving-size pieces

1 rabbit, cut into serving-size pieces

1½ pounds venison sausage, cut into bite-sized pieces (see page 41)

1 cup flour

4 cups chopped onions

2 cups diced celery

2 cups chopped green bell peppers

1 garlic clove, chopped

8 cups beef or venison stock (see page 30)

Cayenne pepper, to taste

1 to 2 teaspoons salt, or to taste

1 cup chopped green onions

1 cup chopped fresh parsley

Filé powder to taste (see Note)

In a large stew pot, melt the shortening and sauté the pheasant and rabbit pieces until golden on all sides. Remove from the pot and allow to cool. Remove the meat from the bones. Sauté the sausage in the remaining fat in the pan, then set aside.

To make the roux, bring the fat in the pan to just under spatter temperature. Using a long-handled spoon, carefully add the flour all at once, stirring constantly. After the flour is added, use a whisk to incorporate it into the fat. Maintain the heat and stir constantly until the roux begins to smooth and darken. Continue to cook and stir until a dark golden color is reached. The darker the roux, the stronger the gumbo.

Combine the onions, celery and green peppers in a large bowl. Pour the hot roux over the vegetables and stir to combine. Stir in the garlic. Return this mixture to the pot and cook until the vegetables are tender and a glaze forms on them (about 10 minutes). Return the pheasant, rabbit, and sausage to the pot and cook over low heat. Gradually stir in the stock and bring to a boil. Reduce the heat to a simmer and cook for 1 hour. Season to taste with cayenne and salt. The gumbo may be prepared ahead of time up to this point.

Ten minutes before serving, add the green onions and parsley. Serve over cooked long-grain rice. Filé may be placed on the table for individuals to add their own—¼ to ½ teaspoon per serving is recommended.

Note: Filé is the ground leaf of the sassafras plant. Always use it sparingly, and only when cooking is complete. If it is added to a soup or gumbo during cooking, it will thicken the broth beyond reason. It is available in most gourmet shops.

Serves 8

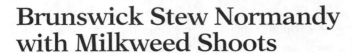

Brunswick Stew Normandy with Milkweed Shoots

1 squirrel

1 rabbit

1 pheasant

1 pound venison, cubed

2 medium onions, coarsely chopped

½ cup sliced green onions or scallions

4 stalks celery, diced, plus some of the young leaves, sliced

1 (10-ounce) package frozen lima beans

1 cup chopped carrots

1 (16-ounce) can stewed tomatoes, with juice

1 cup frozen peas

1 cup frozen corn

½ cup chopped young, tender milkweed shoots
   or white asparagus

½ teaspoon oregano

½ teaspoon Bell Poultry Seasoning

½ teaspoon pepper

Salt, to taste

2 tablespoons cornstarch (optional)

½ cup brandy

In a covered Dutch oven, gently poach the squirrel, rabbit, and pheasant in 3 cups of water. Cool, remove the meat from the bones, and cut into bite-sized pieces. Strain and reserve the broth. In a large ungreased stew pot, sear the venison quickly over high heat for several minutes to seal in the juices. Add the reserved broth, onions, celery, lima beans, carrots, squirrel, rabbit, and pheasant pieces; cook for 20 minutes at a slow simmer. Add the tomatoes, peas, corn, milkweed shoots or white asparagus, and seasonings. Simmer for another 35–40 minutes, stirring occasionally. Thicken, if necessary, with a paste made of 2 tablespoons cornstarch and ¼ cup cold water. Stir in the brandy just before serving.

Serves 8–10

Fish and Seafood

Game Fish

AFTER VISITING the fish market and paying $4–6 per pound for fish fillets, the average person rushes home to prepare or refrigerate them. How different, though, is our typical stream-side behavior. A late-season trout-fishing experience, shared with me by a noted writer and published in a leading magazine, began, "As the third trout was added to my creel, I realized that the temperature had risen to 80 degrees . . ." I shudder to think of the similar treatment many fish receive before they reach our tables.

Care after the Catch

Every time you set out on a fishing trip, be optimistic: Take along a cooler and some ice. Then, when the action slows, steal a minute to ensure the edibility of your catch by cleaning it properly. As soon as a fish dies, bacteria begin to attack the flesh. It is extremely important, therefore, to eviscerate and de-slime your catch immediately.

Taking it to the cooler as soon as possible and covering it with ice (especially the body cavity) will help preserve that "just-caught" quality. Take a cue from commercial fishermen and use shaved ice. Shaved or cracked ice will cover the body surface of the fish more effectively than will cubes or a block of ice. The fish will cool down faster and retain its flavor.

To get cracked ice in your cooler at streamside, try this trick. Wash out waxed cardboard milk cartons, fill them with water, and freeze. When you go fishing, grab one of these and throw it in the cooler as part of your standard equipment. The block will remain frozen much longer than cubes. When you catch the first fish, smash the container on any hard surface, or rap it with a hammer or a rock on all sides; you'll have instant crushed ice. Once you try this, you'll find yourself using these blocks all year long. Even if you have an ice maker at home, they are a fast supplement in an emergency or for a party.

Before cleaning your fish, rub your fingers with lemon juice and then salt. This prevents the fishy odor from clinging to your hands. Also, the salt makes the fish easier to handle.

Freezing Fish

Any fish not consumed when it is caught may be frozen, but take special care in this process, also. The most important thing is to get the fish frozen quickly. A fish over 4 pounds is hard to freeze quickly enough to preserve the flavor. Thus, it is best to cut large fish into steaks or fillets before freezing. Place the fish pieces on a baking sheet or a metal tray on a well-ventilated, empty freezer shelf. Cover loosely with foil. When the flesh is frozen solid, wrap tightly with a heavy, freezer-weight plastic wrap. Store the wrapped fillets in a heavy freezer bag.

Small fish may be frozen whole in the same manner, until they are solid. Then place them in a container such as a milk carton, fill the container with cold water, and freeze. Freezing small fish in a block of ice has always been regarded as an effective way to preserve them; however, again, the time it takes to freeze is very important. Pre-freezing and then encasing in ice will reduce the time and help to retain the flavor.

If you catch a lunker and want to save it to serve whole for a special occasion, certainly that can be accomplished—many of us have done it for years. Just be aware that you are sacrificing some flavor, and pay special attention to the freezing time. Turn the fish several times during the 3 or more hours required to render it solid, and be sure to place it on a well-ventilated shelf. Large fish should be glazed after they are frozen to protect them from freezer burn (evaporation), because they are difficult to wrap effectively. To do this, after the fish is frozen thoroughly, remove it from the freezer and run it under a trickle of water to coat the entire surface. As the water hits the frozen surface of the fish, it will instantly form a thin glaze of ice. Return it to the freezer. Repeat two or three times and then wrap securely. Use heavy plastic wrap, removing all the air by pulling tightly. Then wrap again in freezer paper. Dating the package helps to remind you when it's time to use the fish. For best results, eat as soon as possible; don't keep fish longer than 3 months.

To thaw fish and preserve the flavor of those catches not protected by being encased in a block of ice, remove from the freezer, pour buttermilk or milk over the fish, and allow to thaw at room temperature. This will help prevent any strong flavors from developing and will keep the fish from drying out as it thaws.

Excellent fish stock may be prepared by simmering the bones and heads of any cleaned fish until the meat flakes from the bone (see page 139). Salmon makes exceptional stock. This is a good way to use the remaining body parts from any large fish that you are cutting into steaks. Fish stocks should be frozen for future use. However, they are best if used within 6 weeks. Use fish stock for sauces, soups, and stews.

Never throw away leftover cooked fish. Remove the bones and skin to make fish stock, and save the flesh for use in salads and chowders. Cooked fish may also be frozen for later use. For best results, do not store cooked flaked fish more than 3–4 weeks in the freezer. Freezing in broth or water helps preserve the flavor.

Smoking Fish

Curing by exposure to smoke is one means of temporarily preserving fish, and of producing an appetizing flavor.

The best fish to smoke are those with a high fat content, such as carp, catfish, salmon, smelt, herring, whitefish, eel, and lake trout. There are four steps in preparing your catch: cleaning, brining, drying, and smoking.

The first step is cleaning the fish. Depending on the species, fish may be gutted and beheaded, halved, filleted, or skinned and cut into pieces. Small fish may be smoked in the round (without cleaning). Fresh fish may also be cleaned and frozen for later smoking.

After cleaning, you are ready for step two, brining the fish. This means steeping the fish in a solution of salt, water, and spices. This process is essential before smoking; it firms the fish by removing moisture. Here are two brine recipes for hot smoked fish:

I	II
1 gallon water	6 gallons water
1 pound salt	4 pounds salt
½ pound sugar	1½ pounds sugar
⅓ cup lemon juice	1½ ounces saltpeter
½ tablespoon onion powder	3 ounces whole cloves (optional)
½ tablespoon seafood seasoning	1 ounce bay leaves (optional)

Recipe I makes enough brine for 4 pounds of fish; recipe II, enough for 20 pounds of fish.

Mix the ingredients well. Submerge the fish in the brine and refrigerate for 12 hours. Remove the fish from the brine and freshen under running water for 10 minutes.

Now you are ready for step three, drying the fish. Pat the fish dry with a cloth. Line a baking sheet with a cloth or paper towel, and place the fish on it in a single layer. Put in the refrigerator to drain for 1–3 hours. Drying increases the keeping quality of the fish and promotes development of the pellicle, a glossy finish of dissolved proteins on the fish.

The last step is the actual smoking of the fish. There are both cool and hot smoking techniques.

Cool-smoked fish require a heavier brine and a smokehouse temperature not over 90°F in which the fish are cooked for 1–5 days. Cool smoking is seldom done, except to preserve fish for long periods.

Hot-smoked (kippered) fish require a smokehouse temperature of 150–200°F, but a shorter cooking time of 4–5 hours. Hot-smoked fish are perishable and must be refrigerated.

For either process, you will need a smokehouse. Your smokehouse may be designed from a large cardboard box, a metal drum, a wooden barrel, or an old refrigerator. The cardboard box is perhaps easiest to obtain; it should be 30 inches square and 48 inches high. Refer to the following diagram and building instructions.

1. Remove one end of the box to form the bottom of the smokehouse.
2. Unfasten the flaps at the opposite end so they fold back and serve as a cover.
3. Strengthen the box, if necessary, by tacking ¾-inch strips of wood onto the outside—vertically at the corners and horizontally across the sides.
4. Cut a door 10 inches wide and 12 inches high in the bottom center of one side. Make one vertical cut and one horizontal cut, so the uncut side serves as a hinge.
5. Suspend several rods or sticks (iron or wood) across the top of the box. Cut holes through the box, so the rods rest on wooden strips. A rack of coarse wire mesh (heavy ½-inch or ¼-inch iron or steel) may replace the rods.
6. Arrange the fish on the rods or rack so they do not touch. The fish may be hung on S-shaped hooks; strung through the gills by rods; split and nailed to rods; or simply laid on the rack. Use regular nails, 8- or 10-gauge steel wires, coat hanger wires, S-shaped iron hooks, and/or round wooden sticks.

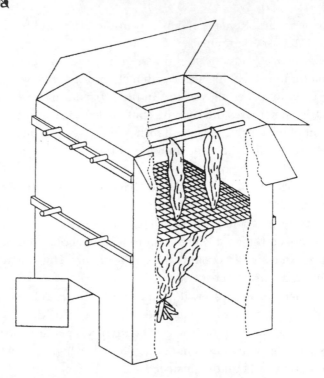

7. Build a fire on level ground with nonresinous (hickory, oak, maple, apple) wood chips or sawdust to produce a light, constant volume of smoke. Never use wood containing pitch, such as pine.

8. Center the smokehouse over the smoldering fire and close the flaps. The danger of fire is minimized if the ventilation is controlled to promote smoke rather than flames. This can be accomplished by closing the flaps to reduce the oxygen intake.

9. Monitor fish temperatures by inserting a meat thermometer into the fleshiest part of the fish. Maintain an internal temperature of about 180°F for kippered fish. (Temperatures exceeding 200°F can cause excessive drying of the fish.)

10. Smoke for 4–5 hours.

Basic Fish Stock

Fish scraps (bones, heads, and backs)
2 or 3 stalks celery
1 large onion
2 or 3 bay leaves

Measure your fish scraps, then put them into a kettle with twice the amount of water. That is, if you have 2 cups of fish bones, add 4 cups of water. Add the celery, onion, and bay leaves. Bring to a boil, reduce the heat, and simmer, uncovered, for 30–40 minutes. Strain and use immediately for soup, or freeze for future use.

Baked Bass
with Sour Cream Dressing

3- to 4-pound whole bass
1 tablespoon butter, melted
½ cup plain yogurt
½ cup reduced-fat sour cream
½ cup chopped onions
½ cup chopped celery
½ teaspoon Old Bay Seafood Seasoning
½ teaspoon basil

Clean, wash, and dry the fish. Preheat the oven to 300°F. Combine the butter, yogurt, sour cream, onions, celery, Old Bay seasoning, and basil. Spread this mixture in the cavity of the fish. Wrap the fish with foil, sealing well. Place on a baking sheet or in a baking dish and bake for 50–60 minutes, or until the flesh flakes easily.

Serves 6

Snappy Pickerel

1 whole pickerel

2 tablespoons tamari (see Note)

¼ teaspoon hot pepper sauce

1 lime, sliced

1 teaspoon grated gingerroot

2 tablespoons butter

1 teaspoon sesame oil

Marinating time: 1–2 hours

Preheat the oven to 325°F. Remove the head and tail from the fish. Split open and lay flat, skin-side down. Sprinkle the flesh with the tamari and hot pepper sauce. Top with the lime slices and gingerroot. Marinate in the refrigerator for 1–2 hours.

Melt the butter in a saucepan over medium heat. Add the sesame oil and heat to combine. Pour over the fish and bake for 15–20 minutes, depending on the size of the fish. The fish is done when the flesh is opaque and flakes easily.

Note: Soy sauce can be substituted for the tamari.

Serves 2–3

Baked Pickerel

1 large pickerel or several small ones
½ cup plain yogurt, drained (see *Note*, page 78)
Juice and zest of 1 lemon

Fillet the pickerel, leaving the skin on. Place the fillet skin-side down in a greased baking dish. Spread the flesh with the yogurt and pour the lemon juice over. Sprinkle the lemon zest over the fish and bake at 350°F for 15–20 minutes, depending on the thickness of the fillets. The fish is done when the flesh is opaque and flakes easily.

Serves 2–3

Whole Baked Pickerel

1 whole pickerel
1 lemon, sliced
4 green onions, chopped
2 tablespoons butter, melted
½ cup orange marmalade

Preheat the oven to 300°F. Remove the head and tail from the pickerel and open the body cavity by cutting through the fish from top to bottom. Lay flat in a greased baking dish, skin-side down. Cover the fish with lemon slices. Top with the green onions. Combine the butter and marmalade and pour over all. Bake for 15–20 minutes, depending on the size of the fish. The fish is done when the flesh is opaque and flakes easily.

Serves 2–4

Spicy Catfish

6 whole catfish, cleaned and skinned
1/2 cup tomato sauce
I ripe tomato, peeled and chopped
I cup Cheesy Italian Dressing (see below)
3 tablespoons chopped fresh parsley
2 tablespoons grated Romano cheese

Preheat the oven to 350°F. Pat the fish dry, inside and out. Combine the tomato sauce, chopped tomato, dressing, and parsley. Brush the fish inside and out with this mixture. Place in a well-greased baking dish. Pour the remaining sauce over the fish and sprinkle with the cheese. Bake for 25–35 minutes, or until the flesh flakes easily. Place the fish under the broiler about 3 inches from the heat and broil for several minutes, until crisp and bubbly.

Serves 6

Cheesy Italian Dressing

1/4 cup vinegar
2/3 cup salad oil
I tablespoon grated Parmesan cheese
I clove garlic, minced
1/2 teaspoon grated onion
1/4 teaspoon red pepper flakes
1/4 teaspoon sugar

Combine all ingredients and shake or blend in a blender until thoroughly mixed.

Catfish Supreme

I pound catfish fillets
4 cups buttermilk
I cup cracker meal
3 tablespoons butter or margarine
¼ cup vegetable oil

Marinating time: 1 hour

Cut the fillets into serving-size pieces. Marinate in the buttermilk, turning frequently, for 1 hour. Remove from the buttermilk and coat with the cracker meal. Heat the butter and oil in a frying pan. Over medium heat, fry the fish to golden brown. Serve immediately on a heated platter.

Serves 4

Catfish with Lemon

8 catfish fillets
Zest of 6 lemons, divided
8 tablespoons butter (I stick) , melted
6 tablespoons vermouth
I clove garlic, crushed
3 tablespoon chopped fresh parsley

Preheat the oven to 375°F, or prepare a fire in the grill. Place half the lemon zest on a sheet of aluminum foil, top with the fish fillets, and cover with the remainder of the zest. Combine the butter, vermouth, garlic, and parsley. Spoon the mixture over the fish and seal the foil package. Cook in the oven or over hot coals for about 20 minutes, depending on the size of the fillets. The fish is done when the flesh is opaque and flakes easily.

Note: If you enjoy the taste of garlic, then by all means invest in a garlic press. I can't believe I did without one all these years.

Serves 6

Northern Pike Cakes with Mornay Sauce

This recipe comes from the excellent Moosehead Lodge in Quebec.

2 cups filleted pike
1 teaspoon Old Bay Seafood Seasoning
1 egg, beaten
1 cup mashed potatoes
2 tablespoons butter
2 tablespoons corn oil
Mornay Sauce (see next page)

Run the pike fillets through a food grinder, using the fine setting. This eliminates any small bones missed in filleting. Combine the ground fish with the Old Bay seasoning, egg, and potatoes. Preheat the oven to 300°F.

Form the fish mixture into cakes about the size of the palm of your hand. Heat the butter and oil in a frying pan, and lightly sauté the cakes in it until golden. Remove immediately and place on a baking sheet. Bake for ½ hour. Serve with Mornay Sauce.

Serves 4

Mornay Sauce

4 tablespoons butter (½ stick)
¼ cup flour
½ cup water
½ cup milk
½ cup grated **Gruyère** cheese
¼ cup grated **Parmesan** cheese

Melt the butter. Stir in the flour to make a roux. Continue stirring over medium heat until the roux is golden and all the flour is incorporated. Slowly add the water and milk, stirring constantly to blend. Bring just to a boil and lower the heat. When the sauce is smooth, add the grated cheeses. Heat just until the cheese melts.

Pike Fillets

Pike is very bony, so this is a good recipe for larger, meatier pike. This recipe will also work well with any lean fish—that is, fish that contain less than 5 percent fat. This group includes trout (except lake trout), flounder, walleye, and pickerel.

I pound pike   *Marinating time: 1–2 hours*
I cup drained yogurt (see *Note*, page 78)
2 cups cracker meal
½ cup vegetable oil

Clean the fish and cut into fillets. Pat the fillets dry and spread with the yogurt. Coat with the cracker meal and refrigerate for 1–2 hours. In a heavy skillet, heat the oil to 350°. Fry the fillets in the oil over medium heat until the cracker meal is golden and the flesh is opaque, usually 2–4 minutes per side, depending on the thickness of the fillets. Drain and place on a heated platter. Serve immediately.

Serves 4

Baked Orange Perch

Low fat

2 pounds perch fillets
1 tablespoon corn oil
1 clove garlic, minced
2 tablespoons lime juice
¼ cup orange juice
Zest of 1 orange
½ teaspoon grated gingerroot

Preheat the oven to 325°F. Arrange the perch fillets in a baking dish. In a blender combine the oil, garlic, and juices. Pour over the fillets. Sprinkle with the orange zest and gingerroot. Cover and bake for 10–12 minutes, depending on the thickness of the fillets. The fish is done when the flesh is opaque and flakes easily.

Serves 6

Parsleyed Perch

2 pounds perch, cleaned and split
3 tablespoons butter, softened
4 tablespoons chopped fresh parsley
⅛ teaspoon Old Bay Seafood Seasoning
Paprika, for garnish
Parsley sprigs, for garnish

Preheat the broiler. Leave the skin on the perch to help retain its shape. Arrange the perch halves skin-side down on a broiler pan. Combine the softened butter, parsley, and seafood seasoning. Spread the fish with the parsley-butter mixture. Broil 4 inches from the heat, for about 4 minutes. Set oven to bake at 300°F and allow the fish to cook for 2–5 minutes longer, depending on the thickness of the fillets. Garnish with the paprika and parsley sprigs. Serve immediately.

Serves 6

Sweet and Spicy Perch

1 cup flour
¼ teaspoon rosemary
3½ to 4 pounds perch, skinned and filleted
½ cup olive oil
1 cup water
½ cup lime juice
¼ cup honey
1 clove garlic, minced
Lime slices, for garnish

Combine the flour and rosemary. Coat the perch in the flour mixture. In a heavy skillet, heat the oil to 370°F and fry the fish, turning once, until browned. Remove the fish and drain on paper towels. Drain the excess fat from the skillet. In a saucepan, mix the water, lime juice, honey, and garlic and bring to a boil. Return the fish to the skillet and pour the liquid over it. Simmer, uncovered, for 5 minutes. Garnish with lime slices and serve immediately.

Serves 6

Limed Muskellunge Steaks

Muskellunge, often referred to as muskie, is a large North American pike. It can weigh as much as 60–80 pounds, and is a favorite game fish in large lakes.

1 muskellunge, cut into 1-inch-thick steaks
1 cup lime juice
Zest of 2 limes
1 cup flour
2 tablespoons butter
⅓ cup corn oil

Marinating time: 2–3 hours

Arrange the steaks in a shallow dish. Pour the lime juice over them and sprinkle with the lime zest. Cover and marinate for 2–3 hours in the refrigerator. Remove the steaks from the juice and dredge in the flour. Heat the butter and oil in a heavy skillet. Shake off the excess flour from the fish and fry until golden on both sides. The fish is done when the flesh flakes easily. Drain on paper towels and serve immediately.

Serves 6–8

Baked Muskellunge with Almonds

This elegant dish is fit for a special occasion.

1 whole muskellunge

Stuffing
4 cups bread cubes
6 tablespoons chopped fresh parsley
¼ cup chopped blanched almonds
1 teaspoon nutmeg
4 tablespoons butter (½ stick), melted

Paste
¼ cup dry vermouth
4 tablespoons butter (½ stick), softened
1 cup ground almonds

Basting liquid
4 tablespoons butter (½ stick), melted
3 tablespoons vermouth

Preheat the oven to 400°F. Cut the muskellunge into two pieces to fit into a baking pan. Combine the bread cubes, parsley, chopped almonds, nutmeg, and melted butter. Gently stuff the mixture into the body cavity of the fish. Combine the ¼ cup vermouth, softened butter, and ground almonds to make a paste. Spread the paste over all the outside surfaces of the fish. Combine the 4 tablespoons of melted butter with the 3 tablespoons of vermouth. Bake at 400°F for the first 15 minutes, basting with the butter-vermouth mixture; then reduce the oven temperature to 325° and bake for approximately 20–30 minutes more, continuing to baste. Test for doneness; the fish is ready when the flesh flakes easily.

Serves 6–8

Broiled Walleye Fillets

2 pounds walleye, filleted
1 teaspoon Worcestershire sauce
Coarsely ground pepper, to taste
3 tablespoons butter, melted
Fish Steak Topping (see below)

Place the fish fillets on a greased broiler pan. Combine the Worcestershire sauce and pepper with the butter and brush on each fillet. Broil 3 inches from the heat for 4–6 minutes, or until slightly browned. Again brush the broiled surface with the butter mixture, then turn the fillets. Brush the uncooked side with the butter mixture and broil 4–6 minutes longer, or until the fish flakes easily. Cover each piece with some of the topping mixture and broil about 1 minute longer, until golden.

Serves 6

Fish Steak Topping

½ cup mayonnaise
½ cup grated Romano cheese
½ teaspoon Old Bay Seafood Seasoning
1 egg white, stiffly beaten

Gently fold the mayonnaise, cheese, and seasoning into the egg white.

Yield: ¾ cup

Mary Taggart's Walleye Tempura with Sweet Onion Sauce

Two 18-inch walleyes should weigh about 4 pounds and will feed four hearty appetites. A good guide is to serve one average-size walleye for every two people. Walleyes usually reach a pound when they are about 14 inches long; 2 pounds at 18 inches. They will generally add at least a pound in weight for every 2 inches thereafter.

2 walleyes (about 2 pounds each)
1 cup peanut oil
½ cup flour
Tempura Batter (see next page)
Sweet Onion Sauce (see next page)

Clean and fillet the fish. Cut the fillets into dollar-bill-size pieces. In a heavy skillet, heat the oil to 350°F. Dredge the fish pieces in the flour, then dip them into the tempura batter. Fry the fish pieces in the hot oil until golden brown and the flesh is opaque and flakes easily. Remove and drain on paper towels. Serve with Sweet Onion Sauce.

Serves 4

Tempura Batter

2 cups flour
½ cup cornstarch
2 tablespoons baking powder
1 teaspoon baking soda
1 egg, slightly beaten
1½ cups cold water

Combine the flour, cornstarch, baking powder, and baking soda. Stir in the egg. Add the water and beat to combine; the batter will tend to be lumpy. Using a whisk, beat until all the large lumps disappear. Keep the batter as cold as possible. The batter may be made a short time ahead and stored in the refrigerator, although eventually the baking soda will lose its power.

Sweet Onion Sauce

½ cup cold water
¼ cup ketchup
2 tablespoons white vinegar
¼ cup dry onion soup mix
2 tablespoons sugar
1 clove garlic, minced
1 teaspoon cornstarch

Mix all the ingredients in a saucepan and heat over medium heat. Stir until the mixture begins to boil. Lower the heat immediately and stir for 3 minutes more, or until the sauce is thickened. Keep warm.

Wonderful Walleye

2 pounds walleye fillets
½ cup chopped green onions
¼ cup apple schnapps
½ cup apple juice
¼ cup lemon juice
Zest of 1 lemon
2 tablespoons butter
1 tablespoon cornstarch
¼ cup heavy cream (see *Note*)
½ cup grated Parmesan cheese
Chopped fresh parsley for garnish

Preheat the oven to 350°F. In a large, buttered baking dish, arrange the walleye fillets in a single layer. Sprinkle with the green onions, schnapps, apple and lemon juices, and lemon zest. Cover and bake for 15 minutes. Reserving the cooking liquid, remove the fish to a heated platter and hold in a warm oven. Strain the cooking liquid and keep warm.

In a small saucepan, melt the butter, mix in the cornstarch, and cook for 2 minutes. Stir in the baking liquid and heavy cream. Cook over medium heat, stirring constantly, until thickened. Pour over the fish and sprinkle with the Parmesan cheese. Run under the broiler until browned. Top with the parsley.

Note: Use evaporated skim milk instead of cream to reduce the fat.

Serves 4–6

Stuffed Steelhead Trout

I large steelhead trout, cleaned
I cup cooked brown rice
I cup diced celery
I cup sliced mushrooms
½ onion, chopped
¼ cup diced pimientos
½ cup yogurt, drained (see page 78)
I (10½-ounce) can condensed mushroom soup
I lemon, sliced

Prepare a charcoal fire or preheat a gas grill. Place the cleaned whole fish on a double layer of heavy aluminum foil. Combine the cooked rice, celery, mushrooms, onions, pimientos, drained yogurt, and mushroom soup. Stuff the cavity with the rice mixture. You'll have some left over; place the remaining stuffing in a baking dish. Top the fish with the lemon slices and seal the fish securely in the foil. Place the foil package on the grill rack and grill over medium heat for 30–45 minutes, depending on the size of the fish. Turn several times. Bake the extra rice stuffing at 350°F for 25–30 minutes.

Serves 4–6

Trout Meunière

This wonderful recipe comes from the New Orleans School of Cooking. It's a great dish for a special occasion, and worth every calorie.

Pecan Butter

2 cups pecans

I pound butter (4 sticks), softened

2 tablespoons Worcestershire sauce

I tablespoon lemon juice

4 trout fillets (8 to 10 ounces each)

Old Bay Seafood Seasoning

½ cup flour

I cup milk

I egg

½ cup vegetable oil

New Orleans Meunière Sauce (see next page)

Preheat the oven to 250°F. Spread the pecans on a baking sheet and roast for 1 hour, stirring occasionally, until golden. Chop and reserve ½ cup for garnish. Pulverize the remaining 1½ cups pecans in a food processor until fine. Add the butter, Worcestershire sauce, and lemon juice, and mix thoroughly. (The pecan butter can be prepared up to this point and stored in the refrigerator for several weeks.)

Sprinkle the fish lightly on both sides with Old Bay seasoning. Combine the flour with ½ teaspoon of Old Bay, mixing thoroughly. Beat together the milk, egg, and ¼ teaspoon of Old Bay to make a wash. Heat the oil in a heavy frying pan. Dredge the fillets in the flour mixture, dip into the egg wash, and then into the flour again. Immediately fry in the oil until golden brown on both sides. Remove the fish from the pan, drain well on paper towels, and place on a serving plate. Spread with the pecan butter and cover with New Orleans Meunière Sauce. Top with a sprinkling of the reserved chopped roasted pecans.

Serves 2

New Orleans Meunière Sauce

2 tablespoons butter
2 tablespoons flour
1 ¼ cups fish stock (see page 139)
3 tablespoons Worcestershire sauce
1 ½ teaspoons lemon juice
1 teaspoon Old Bay Seafood Seasoning

In a small saucepan, melt the butter and add the flour, stirring to make a roux. Cook over medium heat for 2–3 minutes, then add the stock, Worcestershire sauce, lemon juice, and Old Bay seasoning. Cook 2–3 minutes more, until thickened.

Grilled Lake Trout

My son Scott often pulls beautiful trout out of Lake Wallenpaupack, and we enjoy them prepared simply, as in this recipe. The flesh is very pink, almost like salmon, and it is a mild, delicious treat. Served with charcoal-roasted potatoes and ears of corn, this makes a summer meal worth remembering.

1 lake trout
2 lemons, sliced
1 medium onion, sliced
Coarsely ground pepper, to taste

Build a charcoal fire or preheat a gas grill. Wash and clean the fish thoroughly. Fill the body cavity with the lemon and onion slices, and sprinkle with the pepper to taste. Wrap the fish in foil and place on the grill. If your grill has a cover, close it and regulate the heat so that it is not flaming. Turn several times, allowing the fish to cook for 30 minutes to 1 hour, depending on the size. The flesh should fall apart easily when the fish is cooked.

Serves 2–4

New Orleans School of Cooking Blackened Redfish

Blackened redfish helped to gain Paul Prudhomme his fame. Owner of K-Paul's Kitchen, one of New Orleans' most famous restaurants, chef Prudhomme has taken his Creole cooking "on the road," introducing this unusual food to San Francisco and New York. He has several excellent cookbooks on the market, and most gourmet stores stock his seasonings.

4 (10- to 12-ounce) boneless redfish fillets
½ cup K-Paul's Blackened Redfish Magic
1 pound butter (4 sticks), melted (divided)
1 lemon, cut into 4 wedges

Generously season both sides of the fish with K-Paul's Magic and dip into 1 cup of the melted butter. Heat a cast-iron skillet to white-hot and place the fish in it skin-side up. Cook on the first side for about 1½ minutes, or until well charred. Turn the fish and cook for about 3 minutes more, until the thickest portion of the fish can be broken off and flaked. Serve with the remaining cup of melted butter and the lemon wedges.

Serves 4

Poached Salmon

Recipes in this book that call for cooked fish require fish that has been prepared in this manner. Strain and reserve the cooking liquid for use in soups and casseroles or add it to Fish Stock (see page 139). Leftover cooked salmon may be used in salads, casseroles, and mousses.

I whole salmon, cleaned
Water
Cheesecloth

Wipe the salmon with a damp cloth and place in the center of a square of cheesecloth. Bring up the four corners of the cloth and tie together at the top. Bring a pot of water to a boil. Holding on to the knot in the cheesecloth, lower the salmon into the boiling water. Bring back to a boil, then lower the heat, cover, and simmer for 20–30 minutes, depending on the size of the salmon. The fish is cooked when the flesh flakes easily.

Steamed Salmon

I whole salmon, cleaned
¼ cup dry vermouth
I cup water or more, depending on size of pot
I clove garlic
I small onion, quartered

Wipe the fish with a damp cloth and place it on a square of cheesecloth. Bring up the ends of the cloth and tie so you can lift the fish out of the pot in one piece. Make a steaming rack by putting a wire rack or an inverted baking dish in the bottom of a large pot or roasting pan. Pour the vermouth into the pot and add enough water to fill the pot 2 inches deep. Add the garlic and onions and bring to a boil on the stove top. When the water is at a rolling boil, lower the fish onto the rack and cover the pot.

Do not reduce the heat. Steam for 1 minute per ounce for a small fish, 2 minutes per ounce for fish more than 2 inches thick. The fish is cooked when it flakes easily. Reserve the cooking liquid for later use in fish stock.

Salmon Rémoulade

Refrigerate this rémoulade for 2–3 hours to bring it to its peak of flavor. It makes an elegant appetizer, a light luncheon entrée, or a cold summer dinner.

4 tablespoons light oil
2 tablespoons white wine vinegar
2 teaspoons paprika
¼ teaspoon cayenne pepper
2 tablespoons Dijon mustard
½ cup chopped celery heart with leaves
2 tablespoons chopped green onions
**½ to ¾ cup cooked salmon,
    boned and flaked (see page 158)**
Mixed lettuces

Combine the oil, vinegar, paprika, cayenne, and mustard in a blender. Blend at high speed until light in color and foamy. Place the celery, onions, and salmon in a bowl and stir in the dressing. Cover and refrigerate for at least 30 minutes, preferably 2–3 hours. Clean the lettuces and divide among salad plates. To serve, spoon the rémoulade on top of the lettuce.

Serves 4 as an appetizer; 2 as a light entrée

Salmon Pasta Supreme

This is a very rich, elegant way to serve salmon.

8 tablespoons butter (1 stick)
4 ounces cream cheese, at room temperature
1 large or 2 small cloves garlic
1 cup fish stock (see page 139)
1½ cups cooked, chunked, boned salmon (see page 158)
1 (16-ounce) box linguine
3 tablespoons olive oil
Fresh parsley for garnish

Melt the butter in a heavy pot and add the cream cheese. Stir until the cheese begins to break down. Add the garlic and continue to blend. Pour in the fish stock and heat just to boiling, stirring constantly. When the cream cheese is blended into the butter and stock, lower the heat and add the salmon. Simmer for 15 minutes, stirring gently, being careful not to break up the salmon chunks too much. Remove the garlic cloves.

Cook the linguine according to the package directions. Drain and toss with the olive oil. Ladle the salmon sauce over the linguine and garnish with the parsley.

Serves 4

Salmon Shells

2 cups cooked, flaked salmon (see page 158)

2 cups ricotta cheese

½ cup grated Parmesan cheese

3 tablespoons butter

3 tablespoons flour

½ teaspoon salt

Dash pepper

¼ teaspoon nutmeg

1 cup cream or milk

1 cup cooked, drained, and chopped spinach

12 large pasta shells, cooked

½ cup grated Locatelli cheese

Preheat the oven to 350°F. Combine the salmon, ricotta, and Parmesan, and set aside. Melt the butter and blend in the flour, salt, pepper, and nutmeg. Add the cream (or milk) gradually and cook until thick and smooth, stirring constantly. Add the chopped spinach to the sauce. Pour the sauce into a well-greased baking dish. Fill the cooked pasta shells with the salmon mixture and arrange in a single layer over the spinach sauce. Sprinkle with the Locatelli cheese and bake for 30 minutes. Garnish with the parsley.

Serves 4

Oriental Salmon

Low fat

2 pounds salmon steaks, cut
  1 ½ inches thick

½ cup soy sauce

½ cup cornstarch

½ cup flour

¼ teaspoon pepper

¼ cup light corn oil

1 teaspoon sesame oil

2 cups chopped celery

1 medium onion, sliced into rings

1 red bell pepper, cut into rings

1 green bell pepper, cut into rings

1 cup sliced mushrooms

Marinating time: 1 hour

Arrange the salmon steaks in a dish and pour the soy sauce over them. Marinate for 1 hour at room temperature, turning several times. Combine the cornstarch, flour, and pepper. Lift the steaks out of the soy sauce (reserve the marinade) and dredge them in the flour mixture. Heat the oils in a skillet and brown the steaks quickly. Preheat the oven to 350°F. Place the browned steaks in a large, well-greased casserole. Steam the celery, onions, peppers, and mushrooms until almost tender. Put the vegetables on top of the salmon and add ¼ cup of the soy marinade. Bake for 30 minutes, or until the flesh is opaque and flakes easily.

Serves 4

Salmon in Cream Sauce

2 pounds salmon fillets
½ teaspoon white pepper
½ cup sour cream
½ cup yogurt
½ teaspoon celery seed
1 onion, cut into rings
¼ cup chopped fresh parsley

Preheat the oven to 350°F. Remove the salmon skin and sprinkle the fillets with pepper. Place the fillets in a shallow, well-greased baking dish. Combine the sour cream, yogurt, and celery seed and pour over the fillets. Top with the onion rings and sprinkle with the parsley. Bake for 30 minutes.

Serves 4

Rosemary Salmon

Low fat

2 pounds salmon steaks   *Marinating time: 2 hours*
½ teaspoon cayenne pepper
2 teaspoons rosemary leaves
2 tablespoons white wine vinegar
3 tablespoons olive oil

Sprinkle the salmon steaks with the cayenne, cover, and refrigerate. Combine the rosemary, vinegar, and oil, and let stand at room temperature for 1 hour. Pour over the cold steaks and marinate at room temperature 1 more hour. Grill or broil about 3 inches from the heat source, basting frequently with reserved marinade, for 5–8 minutes, or until slightly brown. Turn, baste, and cook for 6–7 minutes more, until the fish flakes easily.

Serves 6

Curried Salmon

*A salmon run is an exciting spectacle and can result in an angler's
freezer overflowing with fish. To preserve the delicious flavor,
freeze cleaned salmon for several hours or until firm, then glaze in
several layers of ice (for complete instructions, see page 135).*

½ **pound mushrooms, sliced**

1 **cup long-grain white rice**

1 **(10½-ounce) can mushroom soup**

1 **(8-ounce) can tomato sauce**

½ **cup milk**

2 **tablespoons tomato paste**

2 **cups cooked, chunked, deboned salmon (see page 158)**

4 **tablespoons sherry**

1 **teaspoon curry powder (see Note)**

Steam the mushrooms in ¼ cup water over low heat until cooked
through. Reserve the liquid. Cook the rice according to package directions, using the reserved mushroom liquid as part of the water. Add the
mushrooms to the cooked rice and keep warm. In a saucepan, combine
the mushroom soup, tomato sauce, milk, and tomato paste. Heat through,
stirring to blend. Add the salmon, sherry, and curry powder, and stir gently to combine. Simmer for 3–4 minutes, until heated through. Serve over
the rice and mushrooms.

Note: Curry powder is actually a combination of spices, often including coriander, turmeric, cardamom, cinnamon, red and black pepper, cumin, mace, chilies, nutmeg, fennel, saffron, and caraway. It was
widely used in medieval times to season game. Add a pinch of curry to
scrambled eggs, cream soups, and sauces.

Serves 4

Salmon Rice Salad

2 cups cooked rice
¾ cup Italian Salad Dressing (see below)
1 tablespoon lemon juice
¾ teaspoon curry powder
4 green onions, sliced thin
1 cup chopped celery
1 cup cooked, chunked, and boned salmon (see page 158)
2 hard-cooked eggs, grated
Paprika

Combine the rice, salad dressing, and lemon juice. Stir in the curry powder and mix well to blend. Add the onions and celery and stir well. Gently fold in the salmon. Top with the grated egg and sprinkle with paprika.

Serves 4

Italian Salad Dressing

⅓ cup salad oil
⅓ cup water
¼ cup white vinegar
1 clove garlic, minced
½ teaspoon grated onion
½ teaspoon parsley
¼ teaspoon oregano
¼ teaspoon basil

Shake or blend the ingredients until thoroughly mixed.

Yield: 1 cup

Oriental Fish Steaks

2 pounds rich fish steaks (salmon, king mackerel, tuna, pompano)

Marinating time: 2 hours

½ cup lime juice

Zest of I lime

¼ cup soy sauce

Grated gingerroot, to taste

2 tablespoons sesame oil

I tablespoon lemon juice

½ teaspoon oregano

½ teaspoon basil

½ teaspoon pepper

I clove garlic, minced

Place the steaks in a single layer in a shallow dish. Combine the remaining ingredients and pour over the fish. Marinate in the refrigerator for 1 hour. Turn the steaks and marinate for another hour. Preheat the broiler. Remove the fish from the marinade, reserving the marinade. Place the fish on a well-greased broiler pan. Broil about 3 inches from the heat source for 4–5 minutes. Turn carefully and brush with the reserved marinade. Broil for 4–5 minutes longer, or until the fish flakes easily.

Note: Placing a little water in the bottom of broiler pan—just enough to cover—will eliminate any odor from the juices dripping onto the hot pan.

Serves 6

Florida Seviche

*Don't be put off by the thought of raw fish! The citrus juice used
in preparing seviche firms the connective tissue of the fish, acting
just as heat does on protein. The fish turns from translucent to a
white "cooked" look. One of the benefits of testing recipes for this
cookbook was that I was introduced to the wonders of seviche,
civiche, or ceviche—however you spell it and whatever fish you
use, it's great!*

*My gourmet cooking group occasionally has a potluck night.
Last summer we met on my deck for dinner. I decided to prepare
this seviche, which was a favorite of mine in Guatemala. I was
sure my contribution would be unique, an unusual dish perfect
for a summer evening. However, my good friend and fellow
culinary professional Charlotte Zartman also brought seviche!
We enjoyed one as an appetizer and the other as an entrée.
Use only very fresh fish from clear, unpolluted water for seviche.*

**1 pound red snapper, redfish,
  or salmon**   *Marinating time: overnight*

1 cup lime juice

8 green onions, including tops, sliced thin

1 very ripe tomato, diced fine

1 medium-hot banana pepper, diced fine

½ cup chopped cilantro

Salt and pepper, to taste

Fillet the fish and cut into small cubes. Cover with the lime juice in a
small crock or glass bowl. Cover well and refrigerate overnight. Drain off
the lime juice and add the green onions, tomatoes, banana peppers,
cilantro, and salt and pepper. Chill, covered, for several hours. Serve with
crackers as a first course.

Serves 4–6

Texas Civiche à la Raney

Serve this dish with a variety of crackers. Mr. Nig Raney, of the
Brazorian News *in Jackson, Texas, calls in the neighbors and*
declares a civiche hour! We made it with Lake Erie salmon, and it
was delicious. For a low-fat dish, eliminate the olive oil.

3 pounds fresh fish (salmon,   *Marinating time: overnight*
snapper, ling, trout)

I cup lime juice

I cup lemon juice

I onion, sliced

3 large tomatoes, chopped fine and drained

6 jalapeño peppers, seeded and chopped

I clove garlic, crushed

4 tablespoons olive oil

Cilantro, to taste (see Note)

Clean, fillet, and cube the fish. Place in a crock or glass container. Cover
with the lemon and lime juices, cover tightly, and refrigerate overnight.
Drain the fish well. Add the onions, tomatoes, jalapeños, and garlic and
mix well. Pour the oil over the mixture and stir to combine.

Note: After growing cilantro and experiencing its wonderful flavor in
Guatemalan cuisine, I now use only the fresh herb (dried cilantro is practically tasteless). Cilantro is available year-round in most supermarkets.

Serves 8–10

South Seas Bluefish

Lemon and lime juices are excellent marinades for rich, oily, or strong fish. The citric acid dissipates the strong fish flavor and renders these fish more delicate to the palate.

1 bluefish   *Marinating time: 4–6 hours*

2 cups fresh lime juice

4 limes

1 lemon

1 orange

Wash and clean the fish. Place in a baking dish and pour the lime juice over it. Marinate the fish in the lime juice, covered, for 4–6 hours in the refrigerator, turning frequently. Reserve the lime juice.

Preheat the oven to 275°F. Carefully remove the zest from the limes, lemon, and orange. Cut the fruit into slices. Using half the slices and half the zest, fill the body cavity of the fish with alternating citrus slices, then sprinkle the zest over all. Use the remaining fruit and zest to cover the top of the fish. Baste with the reserved lime juice, cover with foil, and bake for 1–2 hours, or until the fish flakes easily. The cooking time will vary depending on the size of the fish.

Serves 4–6

Grilled Bluefish

Bluefish is delicious and mild if used immediately. To make this recipe with frozen blues, pour lime juice over the frozen fish to cover; allow it to thaw slowly in the refrigerator, turning frequently. The lime juice reduces the strong flavor of this rich fish that is sometimes caused by freezing.

1 (6- to 7-pound) whole bluefish, cleaned

½ cup lime juice

2 teaspoons dill weed

½ teaspoon tarragon

1 lime, thinly sliced

1 cup carrot sticks, steamed tender

1 medium onion, diced

½ cup sliced celery, steamed

Marinating time: 40 minutes

Score the skin of the fish in a diamond pattern. Pour lime juice over it and marinate at room temperature for 40 minutes, turning once after 20 minutes. Meanwhile, prepare a grill and allow the coals to become white-hot. Discard the juice and pat the fish dry. Sprinkle with the dill weed and tarragon. Lay the lime slices and vegetables on top of the fish, and wrap securely in foil. Grill over hot coals for about 20 minutes on each side, or until the flesh is opaque and flakes easily.

Serves 10

Orange Bluefish

No-fat preparation

2 large bluefish fillets (1 to 1½ pounds each)
1 cup fresh orange juice
1 orange
1 red onion, sliced
2 tablespoons honey

Preheat the oven to 350°F. Arrange the fillets in a baking dish and pour the orange juice over them. Remove the zest from the orange and reserve. Cut the orange into slices and arrange them on top of the fish. Sprinkle with the zest, top with the onion slices, and drizzle with the honey. Bake, covered, for 10 minutes. Uncover, baste, and run under the broiler 4 inches from the heat source for an additional 5–6 minutes. If the fish is still not cooked through, turn off the oven, close the door, and allow to stand another several minutes, until the flesh flakes easily.

Serves 6

Smoked Fish Spread

This spread is delicious served with crackers or bread.

1½ pounds smoked fish (see page 136)
2 teaspoons minced onions
2 teaspoons finely chopped celery
1 clove garlic, minced
2 tablespoons finely chopped sweet pickles
1¼ cups mayonnaise (see *Note*)
1 tablespoon Creole or brown mustard
Dash Worcestershire sauce
2 tablespoons chopped fresh parsley
Parsley sprigs for garnish

Mix all the ingredients, place in a mold, and chill for at least 1 hour. Garnish with parsley sprigs.

Note: Fat-free mayonnaise can be used.

Yield: 3½ cups

Clams

CLAMS CAN BE HARVESTED in several ways, but regulations vary in the waters off every coastal state, so before setting out for a day of clamming, check local fishing rules.

Walk along the tidal flats and beaches at low tide and look for siphon holes shaped like keyholes. Using a special clam trowel, or any good digging device, probe beneath the sand, feeling for a shell. Once you learn to identify the specially shaped siphon hole, this can be an effective method in a productive area.

"Toeing for clams" is another popular method, originally used by Native Americans, who waded into shallow waters feeling for clams with their bare feet. Today you can use an inner tube with a basket or net attached to hold the sea creatures after you find them with your toes. This can be a pleasant way to spend a hot afternoon at the beach. Clam beds are usually found on the bay side of offshore islands.

Strong rakes with long handles for gathering clams can be purchased in most seaside communities. These rakes have a holding-basket-type arrangement that will catch any clams raked up. Standing in waist-deep water, the clammer rakes the bottom and lifts the rake to check the basket. Be sure to hold the rake upright or angled back as it is lifted in order not to spill the contents of the holding basket. Here, also, an inner tube or other floating container is handy to hold the clams as you catch them.

Cleaning Clams

It is important to handle your freshly dug clams properly in order to enjoy them. First, wash off all surface sand with sea water or a solution of ⅓ cup salt to 1 gallon tap water. If the clams are very dirty, they should be scrubbed with a brush.

When the clams are clean, cover them with seawater (or the brine solution) and let them stand for 15 to 20 minutes. This allows the clams to cleanse themselves of sand. The salt water is necessary if the clams are to open and discharge sand. The sand will settle to the bottom of the container. Change the water and let them stand another 20 minutes. During this process, expect quite a bit of noise from these sea creatures. It's amusing to see them "burping" bubbles, sticking out their "feet," and generally causing a commotion. When you see how much material is extracted using this method, it will become routine.

Next, the clams are ready to be shucked or steamed. To shuck hard clams, first wash them thoroughly, discarding any broken-shell or dead clams. To open a hard clam, hold it in the palm of one hand with the shell's hinge against the palm. Insert a slender, strong, sharp knife between the halves of the shell and cut around the clam, twisting the knife slightly to pry open the shell. Cut both muscles free from the two halves of the shell. To serve on the half shell, remove only one half of the shell. To use in other recipes, remove and rinse the meat. Since soft clams and surf clams do not have tight-fitting shells, they are easier to open.

An alternate method is to place the clams, after washing, in a small quantity of boiling water. Cover and steam for 5 to 10 minutes, or until they are partially open. Drain, remove, and wash the meat from the shells.

Another method is to first freeze the clams and then wash them under tap water for several minutes. This removes the sand and causes the shells to open sufficiently wide to permit shucking. This method is probably the easiest and most accepted procedure.

To steam clams, again, wash them thoroughly. Depending on the size of your steamer, place the clams about halfway up the sides of the pot. Add ½–1 cup boiling water (a spaghetti cooker would need ½ cup; a larger steamer, 1 cup). Cover the pot securely and steam at high heat for 5–10 minutes, or until the clams open. Serve hot in the shell with melted butter on the side.

When you steam clams, save the liquid from the steamer pot. Strain through a paper-towel-lined colander and freeze for chowders and fish soups.

Stuffed Clams

This is a good way to use the large chowder clams that are sold commercially for chopped canned clams. Large clams are for sale at little stands all along the Atlantic shore.

1 dozen large clams
6 tablespoons butter (¾ stick)
¾ cup chopped onions
½ cup chopped mushrooms
1 tablespoon flour
½ teaspoon Old Bay Seafood Seasoning
¼ teaspoon oregano
½ cup bread crumbs
Dash garlic powder

Steam the clams; strain the liquid and freeze for use in chowders, or add to fish stock (see page 139). Shuck and chop the clams, removing the stomach area. Wash the shells and set aside. In a saucepan, melt 4 tablespoons of the butter and sauté the onions and mushrooms until the onions are golden. Blend in the flour, Old Bay, and oregano. Add the chopped clams and cook until thick, stirring constantly. Preheat the oven to 400°F. Grease the clam shells with butter. Melt the remaining 2 tablespoons butter and combine it with the bread crumb mixture. Fill the clamshells with the clam mixture and top with the bread crumb mixture. Place the clams on a baking sheet and bake for 10 minutes.

Serves 6

Fish and Clam Chowder

4 to 6 slices bacon, chopped

2 large cloves garlic, minced

I medium onion, chopped

½ cup finely chopped celery

½ cup chopped leeks

½ cup unpeeled, grated carrot

1½ teaspoons chopped fresh parsley

I teaspoon Old Bay Seafood Seasoning

I (28-ounce) can plum tomatoes, cut up

2 cups water or fish stock (see page 139)

12 clams, scrubbed and rinsed, in shells

½ pound halibut, haddock, or snapper, cut into chunks

½ cup minced clams with juice

2 cups clam juice (or two 8-ounce bottles)

2 or 3 sprigs parsley for garnish

Sauté the bacon until crisp and remove from the pan. Add the garlic, onions, celery, and leeks to the bacon grease and sauté until the onions are translucent. Add the carrot, parsley, Old Bay, tomatoes, and water or stock. Bring to a boil. Add the clams in their shells, the fish, the minced clams with their juice, and the clam juice. Return to a boil, then lower the heat and simmer for 15–20 minutes, or until the clams open. The chowder can be served immediately, or refrigerated overnight to allow flavors to blend. However, it must be used within 2 days. Garnish with the crisp bacon pieces and sprigs of parsley.

Serves 6–8

Fish and Seafood

Chincoteague Clam Chowder

After a week in Chincoteague, Virginia, we come home loaded down with clams, crabs, and sometimes, flounder. I freeze the clams right in the shell for later use in soups and chowders.

6 to 8 slices bacon, cut into strips

I cup chopped onions

I cup chopped celery

2 cups diced potatoes

I cup chopped Chincoteague clams (see Note)

I cup clam broth

2 ripe tomatoes, peeled and chopped

4 cups fish stock (see page 139)

I bay leaf

½ teaspoon oregano

½ teaspoon basil

I (6-ounce) can tomato paste

Salt and pepper, to taste

Sauté the bacon until crisp. Remove the bacon from the pan and drain on paper towels. In the remaining bacon grease in the pan, sauté the onions, celery, and potatoes. Add the clams, clam broth, tomatoes, and fish stock, and bring to a boil. Reduce the heat and add the bay leaf, oregano, basil, and tomato paste. Simmer for ½ hour. Adjust the seasonings, adding salt and pepper if desired. Remove the bay leaf. Garnish with the cooked bacon.

Note: Two 6½-ounce cans of minced or chopped clams can be substituted for the fresh clams.

Serves 6–8

New England Clam Chowder

1 pint shucked clams
¼ cup chopped bacon or salt pork
¼ cup chopped onions
1 cup diced potatoes
½ teaspoon salt
Dash pepper
2 cups milk
Chopped fresh parsley, for garnish

Drain and chop the clams, reserving the liquor. Fry the bacon until lightly browned. Add the onions and cook until tender. Add the chopped clams, 1 cup of the clam liquor (see *Note*), potatoes, and salt and pepper. Cook for 15 minutes, or until the potatoes are tender. Add the milk and heat gently. Garnish with chopped parsley.

Note: If the liquor from the clams does not measure 1 cup, supplement with bottled clam juice or fish stock.

Serves 6

Karen's Linguine with Creamed Clam Sauce

This is my daughter Karen's specialty, and she makes it often for her husband Tom. This clam sauce is thicker and creamier than the original Italian version. The cream cheese adds smoothness and a rich quality lacking in plain clam sauce. This sauce also adheres nicely to the pasta, coating it like a rich tomato sauce does.

¼ cup cream

8 tablespoons butter (1 stick)

2 ounces cream cheese, at room temperature

2 cloves garlic, minced

4 tablespoons olive oil, divided

½ cup chopped fresh parsley

1 cup chopped clams

1½ cups clam juice (see *Note*)

1 (16-ounce) box linguine

¼ cup grated fontina cheese (or other sharp Italian cheese)

In a saucepan, combine the cream and butter and heat until the butter melts. Add the cream cheese and lower the heat. Stir until the cheese is blended into the butter and cream. Add the garlic and continue to blend. Stir in 2 tablespoons of the oil and the parsley. Continue to stir until the sauce is smooth, then add the clams and clam juice and simmer gently for 30 minutes. Cook the linguine according to the package directions. Drain, place in a serving dish, and toss with the remaining 2 tablespoons of oil. Ladle the clam sauce over the pasta and garnish with the grated cheese.

Note: Use the liquor from the clams, supplementing with bottled clam juice if necessary to make 1½ cups.

Serves 4

Clams Oregano

2 tablespoons olive oil
2 tablespoons butter
I medium onion, chopped
I clove garlic, minced
I cup bread crumbs
½ cup chopped parsley
2 teaspoons lemon juice
I teaspoon basil
I tablespoon oregano
2 dozen cherrystone clams, on the half shell

Preheat the oven to 350°F. In a small skillet, heat the oil and butter over medium heat. Add the onions and garlic and sauté until softened. Combine the bread crumbs, parsley, lemon juice, basil, oregano, and sautéed onions and garlic. Spread this mixture on the clams, arrange on a baking sheet, and bake for 10 minutes.

Note: This recipe can be prepared ahead and frozen before baking.

Serves 4–6

Crabs

ANYONE WHO FREQUENTS the Atlantic coast of the United States, from Massachusetts to the Gulf of Mexico, is familiar with the blue crab (*Callinectes sapidus*). The blue crab is the source of most of the crabmeat consumed in this country. Fresh crabmeat comes in several qualities: lump, backfin, flaked, and claw. Lump crabmeat means choice large white chunks of body meat—the premium quality. Backfin meat is in smaller chunks, and flaked meat comes from other parts of the crab. Claw meat is darker and comes from the claws, of course. All of these types may be used in recipes calling for crabmeat. Crabmeat is available canned, frozen, and pasteurized in hermetically sealed cans. I prefer fresh-caught crabs, but when they are not available, I use the pasteurized variety. Whenever you buy crabmeat, it's a good idea to pick through it to remove any pieces of cartilage that may have been missed by the professional sorters.

To catch your own crabs off the Atlantic coast, you need just a string, a net, and a chicken neck. Many, many hours can be spent throwing out a neck and string, slowly pulling it in, and netting those delicious morsels as they cling to and feed on the chicken. We usually wind up a visit to the shore with one of us repeating over and over, "Stop! We have enough crabs!" Of course, more sophisticated equipment is available. You can purchase weighted pins to attach to the chicken necks, or wire traps—but all you really need are these simple tools.

One pound of crabmeat will serve four to six, depending on the recipe you use. Fresh crabs can be consumed in prodigious quantities. Allow four to eight per person.

Cooking live hard-shell crabs is an adventure in itself. I have had crabs crawl behind stoves, under beds in an efficiency motel room, and even all over the car on the way home. To cook them, you need a large steamer, a long pair of tongs, and Old Bay Seafood Seasoning. Bring 3–4 inches of water to a full boil in the bottom of the steamer. When the water is steaming, carefully put the crabs in the basket and sprinkle with

Old Bay. I use 2–3 tablespoons on each layer of crabs, which sounds like a lot, but you need a lot of seasoning to permeate the meat inside the shell. Fill the pot half full of crabs—don't overcrowd them (no more than a dozen or so at a time). Cover the pot and steam for at least 20 minutes. Larger crabs (over 6 inches from point to point of carapace) should be steamed for 25–30 minutes.

The long tongs are very necessary because the crabs get quite active as soon as you disturb them, and will immediately try to pinch anything within claws' reach. Once they grab hold, it takes some force to get them loose, and they can hurt.

Along the coast, you can purchase fresh crabs in most fish markets. They are usually cooked, and usually not cleaned. To clean the crab, break off the claws and scrub the shells. Take off the top apron, or carapace, from the top of the crab and discard. Remove and discard the inedible, spongy white gills, bags, and intestines of the body cavity. Extract the meat from the segmented sections with a small paring knife. A 6-ounce crab will yield 1½ to 2 ounces of meat.

I like to eat crabs with lemon juice as they come out of the pot. You may want to purchase the beautiful pasteurized lump crab available in most markets. In any case, I hope you will be motivated to try crabbing.

Cold Crab Dip

Serve this dip with crackers or fresh vegetables.

Salad Dressing (see next page)
I pound cooked crabmeat
2 teaspoons horseradish
I teaspoon Worcestershire sauce
½ teaspoon Dijon mustard
2 green onions, sliced fine

Combine the salad dressing with the crab, horseradish, Worcestershire sauce, mustard, and green onions. Chill.

Serves 6–8

Hot Crab Dip

This dip can be served warm with party breads or crackers. I have included an excellent recipe for homemade rye crackers that are very good with any dip (see page 232). Give them a try.

3 (8-ounce) packages cream cheese
1 teaspoon grated onion
1 teaspoon mustard
½ cup Salad Dressing (see below)
1 pound cooked crabmeat
⅓ cup sherry

Soften the cream cheese in a double boiler over hot water. Add the onion, mustard, and salad dressing and blend well. Stir in the crabmeat and sherry.

Serves 6–10

Salad Dressing

⅔ cup salad oil
¼ cup white wine vinegar
1 small clove garlic, minced
½ teaspoon Old Bay Seafood Seasoning
¼ teaspoon sugar
¼ teaspoon red pepper

Combine the dressing ingredients in a jar and shake, or combine in a blender.

Yield: About 1 cup

Uncle Ed Malone's Maryland Crab Boil

We used this method to steam Austin's first crab. While vacationing on the Outer Banks, Karen and husband Tom took my grandsons Austin and Ethan (5 and 3 at the time) crabbing. Austin landed a whopper and ate it all up that night, thus initiating another crab lover into the clan.

Every Marylander we've ever met has his own different way to boil crabs. This is how our Uncle Eddie does it. You will need a very large steamer pot. Crabs prepared in this manner may be kept for up to 5 days. Marylanders like their crabs hot and eat them right out of the pot. But most people prefer them chilled and served with lots of lemon. Ed cautions: Sort through the crabs carefully before cooking to make sure each is alive. A crab that doesn't move and has an open mouth should be discarded.

2 dozen jimmy (male) crabs
I gallon water
½ cup kosher salt
¼ ground red pepper
¼ cup black pepper

Chill the live crabs for several hours before cooking. This will render the claw meat free of the shell for easier eating. Bring the water to a boil in a large steamer. Add the salt and peppers and stir to combine. Add half the crabs and return to a boil, cover, and cook for 25 minutes. Remove the cooked crabs from the pot and spread on a flat surface at room temperature. Add 1–2 cups more water to the pot, return to a boil and repeat the process for the second dozen crabs. Allow the crabs to cool thoroughly before refrigerating.

Serves 3–4

Simple Sautéed Crab

12 tablespoons unsalted butter (1½ sticks)
3 tablespoons chopped fresh parsley
½ teaspoon Old Bay Seafood Seasoning
2 pounds lump crabmeat

Melt the butter in a heavy skillet. Add the parsley and seasoning. Stir in the crabmeat, trying not to break up the lumps. Cook gently until heated through, 6–8 minutes. Serve in individual ramekins.

Serves 6

Imperial Crab

2 pounds cooked crabmeat
½ cup mayonnaise
2 tablespoons lemon juice
1 teaspoon Dijon mustard
2 green onions, sliced
4 tablespoons butter (½ stick), melted
Old Bay Seafood Seasoning, to taste

Preheat the oven to 450°F. Place the crabmeat in a shallow baking dish. Combine the mayonnaise, lemon juice, mustard, and onions and pour over the crab. Stir gently to blend, being careful not to break up the crab too much. Drizzle the mixture with the melted butter and sprinkle with the Old Bay seasoning. Bake for 7–10 minutes, or until golden brown and thoroughly heated. Serve over rice.

Serves 6

Fishermen's Grotto Crab Salad

This is the salad the kids and I always order at the Fishermen's Grotto in San Francisco, where they use Dungeness crab. At home we make it with blue crabs, and it tastes just as wonderful, although the view is not the same.

1 head lettuce
4 cups crabmeat
Chef's Special Salad Dressing (see below)
1 lemon, cut into wedges
2 tomatoes, cut into wedges
2 hard-cooked eggs, sliced

Wash and tear the lettuce, and divide among four salad plates. Mound 1 cup crabmeat in the center of each plate and pour the dressing over it. Garnish each plate with lemon wedges, tomatoes, and hard-boiled eggs.

Serves 4

Chef's Special Salad Dressing

2 cups mayonnaise
1 ½ cups chili sauce
¼ cup finely chopped celery
¼ cup finely chopped sour pickles
1 teaspoon horseradish
1 teaspoon lemon juice
½ teaspoon Worcestershire sauce

Put all ingredients into a bowl and mix until well blended. The dressing will keep indefinitely if refrigerated.

Yield: 1 quart

Fish and Seafood

Fishermen's Grotto Pasta and Crab

This is an excellent way to use leftover crabs. Remove the meat from the shells and save some of the claws for garnish. Our Italian friends put the split bodies in whole and let them simmer. Most of the meat falls out, and although it's a little messy eating, the bodies impart a good flavor to the sauce.

¼ cup olive or salad oil
½ cup chopped onions
1 teaspoon chopped celery
1 teaspoon chopped garlic
1 teaspoon chopped fresh parsley
1 cup canned tomatoes
1 cup tomato sauce
1½ cups water
2 teaspoons salt
1 teaspoon black pepper
½ teaspoon paprika
1 pound fresh or canned crabmeat
¼ cup sherry
1 pound spaghetti
Grated Parmesan cheese

In a large saucepan, heat the oil over medium heat. Add the onions, celery, garlic, and parsley and sauté until golden brown. Add the tomatoes, tomato sauce, water, salt, pepper, and paprika. Simmer for 1 hour. Add the crabmeat and sherry and simmer for a few minutes more. Cook the spaghetti according to the package directions and drain. Add to the crab sauce and mix well to combine. Pour the pasta onto a serving platter and sprinkle with grated Parmesan cheese. Serve immediately.

Serves 5–6

Preparing Crabs for She-Crab Soup

Unlike most crab soups, she-crab soup has a clear broth and relies on the ovaries of the female crab for its sweet flavor. Female crabs, or sooks, can be purchased as such and are generally less expensive than the male, or jimmy, crabs. As seasoned crabbers know, the female has a round apron on her underbelly, while a jimmy's apron is long and pointed. Restaurants demand jimmy crabs, as they are larger and contain more meat. Sooks have a delightful flavor, however—they are best for soups and casseroles.

To clean crabs, wash and scrub the bodies and claws thoroughly. Turn each crab over on its back and lift off the apron, removing the carapace, or hard back (top) shell. Holding the crab body in your hand with the meat side facing you, look for two little pink sacs, one on each side of the center cavity, and gently remove. Do not squeeze, as these little ovary sacs are very delicate. The ovary sac varies from the size of a pea to the size of a lima bean, depending on the size of the crab. They are the only oval-round, translucent, pinkish part in the cavity, so you can't mistake them for another body part. Reserve these and rinse the crab body under running water, using a brush to remove any loose parts and the spongy white breathing apparatus the watermen call "dead fingers." You now have a cleaned crab and are ready to make soup. Break off the legs and claws and reserve them for garnish.

The less adventurous cook may choose to skip this whole process and begin with pasteurized lump crabmeat available in most markets. Your soup will be noteworthy, but definitely lacking the sweet essence of crab that the ovaries and crab juice impart.

She-Crab Soup

Often we come home from the eastern shore with so many crabs that we can't possibly eat them all fresh. Freezing them in heavy freezer bags permits us to use them later. We also freeze a little container of ovaries. It seems quite silly now, but during our "crabbing" years—when my every minute was consumed with teaching, ironing, cooking, raising teenagers, and writing—I really thought using the ovaries was my original idea. After surfacing from all these duties and walking in the more sophisticated world of fine dining, I was shocked to learn that this is general practice in seafood cuisine.

4 tablespoons butter (½ stick)
I cup finely diced celery
I medium onion, diced fine
½ cup finely grated carrots
I leek, white and tender green parts only, diced fine
2 cups fish stock (see page 139)
½ teaspoon Old Bay Seafood Seasoning
¼ teaspoon basil
½ teaspoon paprika
4 to 6 medium she crabs (sooks), steamed and scrubbed well
I cup fresh lump crabmeat

In a soup pot, melt the butter and sauté the celery, onions, carrots, and leeks. Add the fish stock, Old Bay seasoning, basil, and paprika and bring to a boil. Reduce the heat and simmer for 15 minutes. Remove from the heat and set aside.

Clean the crabs and remove the ovaries (see page 188). Set aside one claw to garnish each serving, choosing the nicest ones. Place the cleaned crabs in a small pot and add 2 cups of water. Simmer, covered, for 10–15 minutes. Remove the crabs and reserve the broth, straining through muslin or paper toweling. Crack the remaining claws over the broth and catch the liquid. Remove the meat from the claws and add it to the broth. Cut the crab bodies in half and split each half. Pull the crabmeat out of the body sections and add to the broth. Discard the feelers and cleaned bodies. The crab broth should measure 1 cup.

Put half of the crab broth into a blender with the crab ovaries. Blend well, and add to the stock mixture. Add the remaining crab broth to the pot and simmer for 5–6 minutes to heat through. Stir in the lump crabmeat just before serving. Place a crab claw in each serving dish for garnish.

Serves 4 as a first course

Hampton Roads Crab Cakes

1 egg
¼ cup finely chopped green bell pepper
2 small scallions, sliced very thin
4 to 5 tablespoons unseasoned cracker meal
1 teaspoon Worcestershire sauce
1 teaspoon lemon juice
1 pound lump crabmeat
2 tablespoons butter or margarine
2 tablespoons corn oil

In a medium bowl, beat the egg slightly. Add the green pepper, scallions, cracker meal, and Worcestershire sauce, and stir to combine. Add the lemon juice. Gently fold in the crabmeat and mix well. Shape into six cakes. Heat the butter and oil in a frying pan. Sauté the crab cakes quickly, just until browned, about 5 minutes on each side.

Yield: 6 crab cakes

Wild
Greens and
Edibles

NATIVE AMERICANS TAUGHT the first settlers much about how to survive on food found in field and forest. Cooking in many areas of the country comes from these humble beginnings. Indian women knew many ways with wild food that are interesting to try today.

The Indians of Cape Cod ate a wild edible that we know as the Jerusalem artichoke. The cigagawunj, or wild garlic, saved many from starvation. It was prolific in an area the settlers later named for it—Chicago.

Indians also ate pigweed, sorrel, evening primrose, dock, and hedge mustard in salad. They used the tender young shoots of the cattail much as we use asparagus. Rocky Mountain beeweed was the Indian's spinach. Venison was often cooked with dandelion and seasoned with maple sugar.

Flowers added zest as well as nutrients to the Native American diet. Milkweed blossoms and buds were added to meat soups for flavor and thickening. They fried the delicate redbud and boiled the buds of at least 15 other flowers, including marigold, clover, and pokewood, to make jams and relishes; and they ate more than 50 varieties of greens.

Their sweet tooth was satisfied by maple sugar and cattail sap candy. Milkweed blossoms were used to sweeten, as was the morning dew that clung to the blossoms. Acorn meal was made by soaking acorns overnight until the shells split open. The kernels were picked out and spread in baskets to dry, then ground into flour. Today we can try sweetening wild strawberries by shaking the early-morning dew from milkweed blossoms over sun-ripened berries. Next time you gather blueberries, line a basket with fresh sweet fern to preserve the wild woods fragrance on the journey home, as our Native American teachers did.

American Indians were inventive and persistent, developing a rich and varied diet seemingly by instinct. Marion and G. L. Wittrock, in a survey for the New York Botanical Garden, state that American Indians ate the berries and fruits of nearly 300 different plants. Little wonder they had so much to teach the European trappers and explorers who settled their land.

Could the average American today exist for a week without his customary food?

Certainly survival in the wild is not likely to be required of most Americans. Taking a cue from our country's original people, however, you can use some of their ancient wild accompaniments to enhance your diet, particularly with wild game recipes.

The recipes that follow reward you with more than taste and nutrition: You will also benefit from the exercise and tranquility to be found while gathering these ingredients. Spring fields yield tender young dandelion leaves, delicate fiddlehead ferns, and mild lamb's-tongue, while streams offer peppery watercress. The warmth of the sun soon ripens the beautiful wild strawberries just as it did for the Indians long ago. Summer brings blueberries, raspberries, blackberries, and grapes as well as edible roots and flowers. More than just a simple solution to hunger, meals prepared with wild foods are a creative challenge. A natural meal prepared with wild game and wild side dishes requires a commitment of love and patience that nourishes the soul as well as the body.

Try some of these recipes, and I hope you will be pleasantly surprised. If you are unfamiliar with wild plants, and this section interests you, consult one of several excellent field guides. I recommend *Stalking the Wild Asparagus*, by Euell Gibbons, *Edible Wild Plants of Eastern North America*, by Merritt Lyndon Fernald and Alfred Charles Kinsey, and *Free for the Eating*, by Bradford Angier.

Fiddleheads

FIDDLEHEADS ARE THE uncurled fronds of several species of edible ferns. Most fiddleheads are consumable; however, the coiled fronds of the brake fern, or pasture brake fern (*Pteridium aquilinum*), and the ostrich fern are the most commonly used, having been eaten by Native Americans for centuries in salads and soups. Hunters would do well to consume raw fern in quantity when stalking deer with a bow and arrow because the deer feed upon these ferns. If the hunter is ingesting the same food as the animal he is stalking, his breath will not betray him. Eating raw brake fern fiddleheads may enable a hunter to approach to within 20 to 30 feet of a deer without his scent giving him away. This Indian trick really works.

Fiddleheads are best eaten when they are 5 to 8 inches high and covered with a rust-colored, fuzzy coating. Break them off as low on the plant as they will snap, and rub off the fuzz between your fingers. Wash in several changes of cold water to remove the fuzz. Mature fern fronds are tough, taste bad, and some may be poisonous, including the pasture brake fern. They are so tough and distasteful, however, that it is not likely anyone would choose to eat them.

After cleaning, blanch fiddleheads in boiling water for a few minutes before steaming. They have a slight almond flavor that gives salads and soups a different, pleasant taste similar to okra. Fiddleheads are very versatile. They may be added to any green vegetable dish, or served steamed and buttered by themselves, like asparagus. They are good stir-fried, and can be added to salads and soups.

Fiddlehead Salad

2 cups cleaned and blanched fiddleheads
2 cups mixed salad greens
I cup peeled and sliced daikon radish
Oil and vinegar, to taste

Steam the blanched fiddleheads until just cooked, 2–3 minutes. Refresh under cold water. Wash the salad greens. Combine the greens, fiddleheads, and radishes, and toss with oil and vinegar to taste.

Serves 4

Fiddlehead Soup

This makes an unusual and elegant first course.

I quart pheasant or chicken stock (see page 68)
2 chicken bouillon cubes
I cup cleaned and blanched fiddleheads
I cup cooked shredded fowl meat of your choice

Bring the stock to a boil and add the bouillon cubes. Reduce the heat and add the fiddleheads. Simmer 3 minutes. Add the meat, heat through, and serve.

Serves 4

Dandelions

MY FRIEND JOHN Laubach tells me that the name dandelion comes from the French *dent de lion*, or tooth of the lion, probably because of its jagged-edged leaves.

Dandelions are very popular here in Benton, and are even sold in our big supermarket. To gather your own, pick only very young leaves growing in shaded areas. The lighter the color, the better the taste. The leaves are best when the plants first emerge in spring, long before the yellow flowers appear. Dandelions also do well indoors in an area with little or no sunlight. The plants are hardy and will thrive all winter, producing pale, almost white leaves. They are a welcome and healthful addition to winter salads, being very rich in iron.

Wilted Dandelions

3 cups dandelion greens
6 slices bacon
⅓ cup white wine vinegar
Salt and pepper, to taste

Use only young tender dandelion leaves. Wash thoroughly, drain, and tear into bite-sized pieces. Dice the bacon and fry until crisp. Remove the bacon from the pan, drain on paper towels, and crumble. Add the vinegar to the hot bacon grease and bring to a boil, scraping the pan to include any bacon bits. Add the greens and toss them in the hot liquid until they are wilted and heated through. Season to taste with salt and pepper, garnish with the crumbled bacon, and serve immediately.

Serves 4

Creamed Dandelions

3 cups dandelion greens
5 slices bacon
½ onion, minced
1 egg, beaten
¼ cup vinegar
2 tablespoons water
2 tablespoons sugar
1½ tablespoons flour
Sliced hard-cooked eggs (optional)

Wash the dandelion greens thoroughly under running water. Cook in an uncovered kettle with plenty of salt until tender. Drain and set aside. Chop the bacon and brown it in the same pot. Add the onions and sauté, stirring until golden. Add the egg, vinegar, water, sugar, and flour to the pot. Heat slowly, stirring, until thickened. Pour the hot dressing over the greens and mix well. Garnish with sliced hard-cooked eggs, if desired.

Serves 4

Dandelion Spinach Salad

2 cups dandelion greens
2 cups spinach leaves, torn
¼ cup balsamic vinegar
¼ cup water
¼ cup olive oil
1 red onion, sliced thin

Wash the dandelion greens and spinach and toss to mix. Chill. In a separate bowl, combine the vinegar, water, oil, and onion slices. Chill for 30 minutes to 1 hour. To serve, toss the greens with the dressing in a salad bowl.

Serves 4

Dandelion Casserole

2 pounds dandelion greens, washed and chopped
½ cup flour
1 cup cream
4 tablespoons butter (½ stick), melted
½ teaspoon salt
Dash black pepper
½ cup grated Swiss cheese
½ cup cracker crumbs

Preheat the oven to 350°F. Arrange the greens in layers in a greased baking dish, sprinkling with flour between each layer. Combine the cream, butter, salt, and pepper and pour over the greens. Combine the cheese and the cracker crumbs. Top the greens with the cheese mixture and bake for 35 minutes, or until bubbling.

Serves 6

Wild Greens and Edibles

Pennsylvania Dutch Dandelions

3 cups dandelion greens
6 slices bacon, diced
⅓ cup white wine vinegar
2 teaspoons cornstarch
3 green onions or wild chives, chopped

Thoroughly wash and drain the dandelion greens and place them in a salad bowl. Sauté the bacon until crisp. Remove from the pan with a slotted spoon, drain on paper towels, and crumble. Add the vinegar to the hot bacon grease in the pan. Reheat until boiling, stirring constantly. Make a paste with the cornstarch and ½ cup water and slowly stir into the vinegar mixture. Simmer until thickened. Pour the hot dressing over the dandelion greens and garnish with the green onions and crumbled bacon. Serve immediately.

Serves 4

Wild Rice

WILD RICE IS NOT a true rice as we know it, but a wild grain that grows in marshy areas. Because it is difficult to harvest, it is very expensive. Should you be fortunate enough to have a source of wild rice available, it is well worth the effort and time to gather enough for a meal. It is also worth the expense to buy wild rice occasionally. One cup of wild rice will feed four people.

Wild rice was a staple of the Ojibwa diet. They called it the "good berry." They set up camp and staked out preserves to delineate individual harvest rights. The grain was harvested from canoes, roasted, and then threshed using a bucket sunk into a hole in the ground. An Indian wearing new moccasins would then balance himself with two poles as he trampled the grain in the bucket. The chaff was blown away by shaking shallow trays of the grain in a gentle breeze. The wild rice was then cooked in venison broth and seasoned with maple sugar.

Wild Rice with Mushrooms

4 cups water

1 cup wild rice

4 tablespoons butter (½ stick)

½ pound mushrooms, sliced

Bring the water to a boil in a saucepan. Wash the rice and slowly add it to the boiling water, being careful not to interrupt the boil. After all the rice has been added, stir, reduce the heat, and simmer, covered, for 35–40 minutes, or until most of the water has been absorbed and the rice is tender. Meanwhile, melt the butter in a skillet and sauté the mushrooms. When the rice is cooked, drain off any excess water and mix with the mushrooms.

Serves 4

Fried Wild Rice

4 cups water
I cup wild rice
2 tablespoons vegetable oil
I tablespoon sesame oil
2 tablespoons soy sauce
I egg, beaten

Bring the water to a boil in a saucepan. Wash the rice and slowly add it to the boiling water, being careful not to interrupt the boil. After all the rice has been added, stir, reduce the heat, and simmer, covered, for 35–40 minutes, or until the rice is tender and most of the water has been absorbed. Drain. Heat the oils over medium heat in a skillet. Add the rice and stir. Pour the soy sauce over and continue stirring until the rice is golden. Slowly drizzle the beaten egg over the rice and stir quickly so that it will cook in the hot rice. Serve immediately.

Serves 4

Wild Rice with Peas and Onions

1 cup water
⅓ cup wild rice
2 tablespoons butter
½ cup chopped onions
½ cup fresh peas
2 teaspoons lemon juice
2 tablespoons minced fresh parsley
4 nasturtium flowers

Bring the water to a boil in a saucepan. Wash the rice and slowly add it to the boiling water, being careful not to interrupt the boil. After all the rice has been added, stir, reduce the heat, and simmer, covered, for 35–40 minutes, or until the rice is tender and most of the water has been absorbed. Melt the butter in a saucepan and sauté the onions for 3–4 minutes. Add the peas and stir for several minutes more, until tender but still crisp. Stir in the cooked rice, lemon juice, and parsley. Simmer until heated through. Remove to a serving dish and sprinkle with torn nasturtium petals.

Serves 2

Sorrel

SORREL, OR SOUR GRASS, has been known and eaten since 3000 B.C. Sorrel tastes slightly sour, as its name implies, with a flavor reminiscent of spinach with lemon. It is widely used in Russia and in Europe. The Troisgros brothers, in Rouen, France, were awarded a third Michelin star for their restaurant's celebrated Poached Salmon in Sorrel Sauce. The French also enjoy it in their classic soup Potage Germiny.

Sorrel grows in great profusion all over the United States. *Rumex acetosella*, often referred to as sheep sorrel, field sorrel, or sour grass, is easy to identify, even for the uninitiated. The plant grows about 8 to 12 inches high and has pale green leaves shaped like arrowheads. This plant grows from early spring through summer, and in some areas even produces a fall crop. Look for sorrel in fields, along roadsides, in gardens, and lawns. The leaves are small, between one and four inches long, and have a soft texture. For further information on identification, consult a field guide to edible plants.

To prepare sorrel, remove the stems and wash the leaves under cold running water. Cook as you would spinach, with just the water that clings to the leaves. A pound of sorrel will reduce in a blender to ½ to ¾ cup of puree. The resulting puree can be frozen for up to 3 months for later use.

French country cooking relies heavily on sorrel, especially in soups and omelets. Sorrel can also be added to egg and fish recipes for a refreshing variation. Add 1 cup of julienned sorrel leaves to cream soups; or try adding it as a garnish to hot soups, letting the leaves "melt" into the soup 1 or 2 minutes before serving.

Poached Flounder in Sorrel Sauce

4 cups water
¼ cup dry white wine
2 green onions, chopped
1 carrot, julienned
1 celery rib, with leaves, diced
1 bay leaf
1 large parsley sprig
8 black peppercorns
2½ to 3 pounds flounder fillets
Salt and pepper, to taste
Sorrel Sauce (see next page)
Chopped fresh chives and sorrel leaves, for garnish

In a pot, combine the water, wine, onions, carrots, celery, bay leaf, parsley, and peppercorns. Bring the mixture to a boil, then reduce the heat and simmer for 20 minutes.

Preheat the oven to 325°F. Clean and dry the flounder fillets and season with salt and pepper. Place in a single layer in a baking dish. Pour in the wine-and-vegetable mixture. Cover the dish with foil, and perforate to let steam escape. Bake for ½ hour, or until the fish flakes easily but still feels firm. Lift the fish from the liquid, place it on a serving platter, and allow to cool. Cover the cooled fish with the chilled Sorrel Sauce, and refrigerate until serving. Garnish with chives and sorrel leaves.

Serves 4–6

Sorrel Sauce

This sauce can be prepared one or two days ahead of time and refrigerated until serving.

1 cup water
Salt, to taste
2 cups washed sorrel leaves
1 cup washed spinach leaves
2 eggs
2 teaspoons Dijon mustard
2 teaspoons dry white wine
1 cup peanut oil
3 tablespoons minced green onions
Pepper, to taste

In a saucepan, bring the water to a boil and add salt to taste. Add the sorrel and spinach leaves and cook for 2–3 minutes. Drain thoroughly, pressing out all moisture. Chop finely and reserve.

In a blender or food processor, combine the eggs, mustard, and wine and blend until smooth. Continuing to process, add the peanut oil, a small amount at a time, until the mixture is thick and smooth. Add the spinach-and-sorrel mixture and the onions, and blend again. Season to taste with salt and pepper. Chill.

Yield: 2 cups

Watercress

EUELL GIBBONS DESCRIBED watercress as the "king of wild salad greens." Watercress has a pungent, zesty flavor that adds dimension to any salad. It is easily identified by its bright green, notched leaves, which appear in streams and brooks in early spring. Make sure to gather cress only from fresh, clean, flowing water, and to pick the leaves growing just above the waterline.

Watercress Pinwheels

1 loaf unsliced white sandwich bread
1 cup watercress, washed and finely chopped
1 (8-ounce) package cream cheese, softened
Pepper, to taste

Slice the bread lengthwise into ½-inch-thick slices. Remove the crusts. Combine the watercress, cream cheese, and pepper. Spread ¼ cup of this mixture on each slice. Roll up each slice, starting from the narrow end. Wrap each slice in plastic wrap, sealing tightly. Chill until firm. Unwrap each roll and slice into ½-inch-thick pinwheels.

Yield: 24 pinwheels

Watercress Cheese Ball

1 (8-ounce) package cream cheese, softened

2 ribs celery, finely chopped

2 tablespoons mayonnaise

1 teaspoon olive oil

1 teaspoon vinegar

Pinch of saffron

1 bunch watercress, cleaned and chopped

Mix the cream cheese, celery, mayonnaise, oil, vinegar, and saffron in a blender or food processor until thoroughly combined. Form into a ball. Roll in chopped watercress to cover. Chill, then serve with crackers.

Serves 6–8 as an appetizer

Watercress Dip

1 (4-ounce) package cream cheese, softened

¼ cup chopped watercress

2 tablespoons mayonnaise

2 teaspoons minced leek

1 teaspoon grated onion

Dash Worcestershire sauce

Stir all of the ingredients together. Serve with fresh vegetables or on crackers.

Yield: ½ cup

Watercress Salad

1 large bunch watercress
½ cup bean sprouts
¼ cup sliced radishes
3 green onions, chopped
¼ cup balsamic vinegar
¼ cup water
¼ cup olive oil
1 hard-cooked egg, sliced

Clean and stem the watercress, and toss with the bean sprouts, radishes, and green onions. Whisk together the balsamic vinegar, water, and oil to make a dressing. Toss the salad with the dressing, and garnish with the sliced egg.

Serves 4

Cream of Watercress Soup

1 bunch watercress, cleaned
4 tablespoons butter (½ stick)
1 cup chopped leeks
5 medium potatoes, peeled and diced
2 cups chicken stock
2 cups water
1 pint heavy cream

Reserve some perfect watercress leaves for garnish. Chop the remaining watercress, or process in a food processor. Melt the butter in a soup kettle over medium heat. Sauté the leeks until heated through. Add the watercress and potatoes, and cook until the potatoes are translucent. Add the chicken stock and water and bring to a boil. Continue to boil for 5 minutes. Remove from the heat, cool slightly, and blend or process until smooth. Return to the heat, add the cream, and warm to serving temperature. Garnish with the reserved watercress leaves. Serve immediately.

Serves 6

Watercress Soup

2 cups water
1 teaspoon Old Bay Seafood Seasoning
½ large leek, diced
½ cup bamboo shoots
4 tablespoons butter (½ stick)
2 cups chicken stock
1 cup chopped watercress
1 egg, beaten

In a large saucepan, combine the water, Old Bay seasoning, leeks, bamboo shoots, and butter and simmer for 15 minutes. Add the stock and heat through. Add the watercress and heat to boiling. Drizzle in the egg and heat to serving temperature, stirring constantly.

Serves 6

Flowers

I LIKE TO RAISE edible flowers in pots on my deck, where I can enjoy their beauty until it's time to cook. Edible flowers add not only taste and color to a dish, but also excitement. I love to garnish with them—nasturtiums on a plate of fruit for breakfast, violets gracing a bed of greens—and I love to cook with them, as well. Use only fresh flowers grown in an organic garden (free of chemical pesticides and fertilizers) and wash them well to remove dust and dirt. Store flowers in the refrigerator if you must hold them for any length of time.

Gorgonzola, Ramp, and Nasturtium Salad

I love to garnish with nasturtium flowers. Float one on a drink, place a few atop a fruit salad, or garnish a fillet of fish with buds.

1 head **Boston lettuce**

2 **navel oranges**

2 **ramps (wild leeks)**, julienned

¼ cup **Gorgonzola**, crumbled

6 **nasturtium petals**, torn into pieces

4 whole **nasturtium flowers**

Wash, dry, and tear the lettuce, then divide it among four chilled salad plates. Cut the peel from the oranges and slice them thinly. Place two orange slices on each plate. Lay the julienned ramps across the oranges and sprinkle with the Gorgonzola and the nasturtium petals. Garnish with the whole flowers. Serve with your favorite oil-and-vinegar dressing.

Serves 4

Spinach and Violet Salad

4 cups small spinach leaves, washed well and dried

2 pink grapefruit, peeled and with pith cut away

2 small fennel bulbs, sliced thin crosswise

4 teaspoons red wine vinegar

I tablespoon fresh pink grapefruit juice

¼ teaspoon Dijon mustard

Pepper, to taste

2 tablespoons olive oil

20 fresh purple violets (see *Note*)

Divide the spinach among four chilled salad plates. Cut the grapefruit into thin slices and arrange on top of the spinach. Place some fennel slices on one side of each plate. In a small bowl, whisk together the vinegar, juice, mustard, and pepper to taste. Add the oil in a stream, whisking until the dressing is emulsified. Pour over the salads, arrange the violets decoratively on top, and serve immediately.

Note: Violet buds and the tender young leaves are a distinctive addition to any salad.

Serves 4

Jo Natale's Squash Blossoms

What better way to curb a raging crop of zucchini than to eat the blossoms?

2 dozen squash flowers
2 eggs
½ cup milk
I cup flour
I teaspoon baking powder
¼ teaspoon salt
½ teaspoon vanilla
I teaspoon corn oil, plus more for frying

Pick the flowers from the vines of zucchini or winter squash first thing in the morning, when they have just opened. Remove the stamen and pistil from each. Rinse, blot dry, and refrigerate until ready to use. Beat the eggs and stir in the milk. Sift together the flour, baking powder, and salt, and beat into the egg mixture. Beat in the vanilla and the oil, and stir well to combine. Pour about 1 inch of oil into a heavy skillet and heat to 350°F. Gently dip the flowers in the batter and drop them into the oil, being careful not to crowd them or to lower the temperature of the oil. Cook for about 1 minute on each side, or just until the batter is golden. Drain on paper towels and serve immediately.

Serves 4

Marigold and Broccoli Cavatelli

3 tablespoons olive oil

4 garlic cloves, chopped

1 head broccoli, chopped

2 cups chicken broth

1 pound homemade or frozen cavatelli

4 tablespoons butter (½ stick)

Petals of 3 fresh marigolds

4 whole marigolds, for garnish

½ cup grated Parmesan cheese

In a wok or frying pan, heat the oil and sauté the chopped garlic. Before the garlic browns, add the broccoli and stir-fry quickly. Add the broth to cover the broccoli and cook over low heat until tender. Cook the cavatelli to desired doneness, drain, and toss with the butter. Pour the broccoli mixture over the pasta and top with the marigold petals. Garnish with the whole marigolds. Pass the cheese at the table.

Serves 4

Marigold Cheese Spread

3 or 4 fresh marigold flowers

1 (8-ounce) block cream cheese, softened

Wash and shred the marigold petals. With a fork, blend the petals into the softened cheese. Refrigerate until firm. Garnish with a whole flower if desired. Serve with crackers or sliced rounds of toasted French bread.

Serves 6–8 as an appetizer

Lasagna Rolls with Pickled Nasturtium Buds

1 pound lasagna noodles

½ pound mushrooms, sliced

1 cup ricotta cheese

½ cup pickled nasturtium buds, drained

1 small can pitted black olives, sliced

2 cups Spring Marinara Sauce (see page 25)

¼ cup Parmesan cheese, grated

Cook the lasagna noodles according to package directions. Meanwhile, microwave or sauté the mushrooms until half done, and drain well. Mix together the ricotta, nasturtium buds, and the mushrooms until blended. Preheat the oven to 375°F. Cut each noodle in half. Place a dollop of cheese mixture on one end of each noodle. Top with olive slices and roll up jelly–roll style. Place the rolls seam-side down in a baking dish. Top with the Spring Marinara Sauce. Bake for 35–40 minutes, or until heated through. Sprinkle with the cheese.

Serves 4

Pickled Nasturtium Buds

This recipe comes from Rodale's Basic Natural Foods Cookbook *(Rodale Press, 1984).*

1 cup unopened nasturtium buds
¼ teaspoon fennel seeds
¼ teaspoon cumin seeds
¼ cup water
3 tablespoons white vinegar
3 tablespoons lemon juice
1 teaspoon honey

Scald a 1-cup jelly jar and a canning lid band to sterilize. Pack the nasturtium buds, fennel seeds, and cumin seeds into the jar. Bring the water, vinegar, lemon juice, and honey to a boil. Meanwhile, stand the jar in a pan of hot water. Pour the boiling liquid over the buds, leaving a half-inch space at the top of the jar. Screw on the canning lid, cool the jar on a wire rack, and store in the refrigerator for at least 1 week before using, to allow the flavors to blend. Use within 2 months.

Yield: 1 cup

Flower Ziti with Toasted Pine Nuts

This is an adaptation of a wonderful Italian dish I prepared for a group of friends from Guatemala while vacationing at the Puig residence in St. Thomas, Virgin Islands. Ingrid Puig and her mother, Joan Bonatti, are a dear part of my Guatemalan family, and appreciate adventurous cuisine.

Select only perfect nasturtium flowers for garnish, and, of course, flowers that have been grown in a pollution-free environment.

2 tablespoons olive oil

1 clove elephant garlic, chopped

2 heads cauliflower, stems removed
   and separated into florets

2 tablespoons pine nuts

2 cups chicken broth

1 pound homemade or frozen pasta, preferably ziti

2 tablespoons butter

Petals of 6 nasturtiums

4 whole nasturtiums, for garnish

1/2 cup grated Romano cheese

In a wok or frying pan, heat the oil and sauté the garlic. Before the garlic browns, add the cauliflower. Stir-fry until crisp-tender. Toast the pine nuts in a dry pan on the stove top or in the oven just until they change color and release their nutty aroma (about 5 minutes). Set aside. Add the broth to the wok and cover. Cook over low heat until the cauliflower is just barely tender. Cook the pasta according to package directions in salted, boiling water. Drain the pasta and toss with the butter to coat. Add the nasturtium petals to the cauliflower and stir to combine. Pour the cauliflower mixture over the pasta and top with whole nasturtium flowers and pine nuts. Sprinkle with the cheese. Serve immediately.

Serves 4

Grapes and Berries

A Great Grape

Sir Walter Raleigh reportedly discovered the scuppernong grape in 1584 on Roanoke Island, Virginia. The original vine, once called the Walter Raleigh vine, has become known as the mother vine. Its gnarled trunk is now more than 2 feet in diameter, and the vine still bears fruit.

Scuppernong is an Algonquin Indian word meaning "place of the sweet bay tree." It was in the shade of these trees that the scuppernong grape grew in profusion great enough to render it healthy and producing still. Thomas Jefferson was purported to be a devotee of the scuppernong grape and the rich, amber wine it produced. He planted a number of vines at Monticello and proudly served the jelly as well as the wine.

Try scuppernong jelly on sourdough pancakes. Scuppernong wine is available in most liquor stores. It is a rich, spicy wine—close to a sherry— that would be an unusual accompaniment to or ending for a meal of wild game and greens.

Wild Scuppernong Jelly

I quart scuppernong grapes
Sugar
Jelly jars
Paraffin

Remove the stems from the grapes, then wash and drain thoroughly. Mash the grapes, a small number at a time. In a saucepan, bring the mashed grapes to a boil and boil for ½ hour. Remove from the heat and strain the juice through a jelly bag, discarding the seeds and pulp. Measure the juice, then measure an equal amount of sugar. Return the juice to a boil, and boil for 5 minutes. Add the sugar, stirring until dissolved. Cook rapidly until the mixture sheets off a metal spoon. Ladle the jelly into hot sterilized jars. Let the jelly cool, then seal with a ⅛-inch layer of melted paraffin. When the paraffin has cooled, top with another ⅛-inch layer.

Note: Try this with Concord grapes, too.

Yield: 1½ pints

Wild Raspberry Jelly

3 quarts wild raspberries, red or black
7 cups sugar
2 tablespoons lemon juice
I cup liquid pectin
Jelly jars
Paraffin

Crush the raspberries and strain through a jelly bag or cheesecloth. Measure 4 cups of juice. Combine the raspberry juice, sugar, and lemon juice. Cook over high heat until the mixture boils. Add the pectin, stirring constantly. Remove from the heat and skim. Pour into hot sterilized jars. Cool, then seal with paraffin.

Yield: 10 cups

Wild Raspberry Jelly Roll

5 eggs, separated
I cup sugar, divided
3 tablespoons orange juice
I cup sifted all-purpose flour
I teaspoon cornstarch
¼ teaspoon salt
Confectioner's sugar
I cup Wild Raspberry Jelly (see above)

Preheat the oven to 350°F. Beat the egg whites to soft peaks. Gradually add ½ cup of the sugar, beating constantly until very stiff. In a separate bowl, beat the egg yolks until thick; add the remaining ½ cup sugar gradually, beating constantly until thick. Beat in the orange juice. Fold the egg yolk mixture into the egg white mixture. Sift the flour together with the cornstarch and salt, and stir into the egg mixture. Line an 11 x 16-inch jelly roll pan with wax paper. Grease the paper. Turn the batter into the prepared pan and spread evenly. Bake for 15 minutes. Turn out onto a kitchen towel sprinkled with confectioner's sugar. Peel off the paper and trim the crusts. Roll up the cake, starting at a short side, and allow to cool. When cool, unroll and spread with the jelly, then reroll. Cut into slices to serve.

Serves 4

Wild Strawberries and Cream

It's been said that this dish is so delectable that eating it will make a poet of the lucky diner.

2 cups wild strawberries
2 cups whipping cream
4 hot Sour Milk Biscuits (see below)

Gather and immediately clean and hull the berries. Whip the cream until it is just beginning to thicken. Crush the berries in a large bowl. Layer the berries and the cream in a shallow dish and refrigerate overnight. Serve on hot biscuits.

Serves 4

Sour Milk Biscuits

2 cups flour
2½ teaspoons baking powder
¼ teaspoon salt
¼ teaspoon baking soda
3 tablespoons butter
1 cup sour milk (see Note)

Preheat the oven to 450°F. Sift together the flour, baking powder, salt, and baking soda. Cut in the butter with a fork; stir in the sour milk and mix lightly, until just combined. Turn out onto a lightly floured surface and knead gently. Roll out and cut with a floured biscuit cutter or water glass. Arrange on a lightly floured baking sheet. Bake for 12–15 minutes, or until golden.

Note: To make sour milk, combine 1 tablespoon of white vinegar or lemon juice with 1 cup milk.

Yield: 12 biscuits

Wild Greens and Edibles

Wild Strawberry Freezer Jam

Every summer morning, my daughter Karen and I would spend a morning picking our own berries and the afternoon making this jam.

This jam is as close to fresh berries as anything you can find. Served over cheesecake, on toast, fresh biscuits, or scrapple, or in a parfait with orange brandy, it is absolutely superb. It's well worth the time and effort.

3 cups wild strawberries

5 cups sugar

1 cup water

1 envelope powdered pectin

Jelly jars

Mash the berries in a bowl, then add the sugar slowly, stirring after each addition. Stir occasionally for 20 minutes to dissolve the sugar. Bring the water to a boil and add the pectin. Return to the boil and cook for 1 minute, stirring constantly. Remove from the heat. Add the fruit and stir for 2 minutes. Pour into sterilized jelly jars and screw down the lids. Let stand at room temperature for 12 hours. Invert the jars to redistribute the fruit and allow to stand another 12 hours. Freeze.

Yield: 5–6 cups

Maple Syrup

MAPLE TREES ARE tapped in early spring when the days start to warm but the nights are still cold. Trees should be about 40 years old to be good sugar producers, and most will go right on producing for a century or more. Maple sap is a delicate liquid. It must be boiled down quickly before exposure to sun and air causes bacteria to develop that will mar its sweetness and flavor.

Maple sugar was used by Native Americans to sweeten their food (see Indian Venison, page 20). Today we can use pure maple syrup to sweeten fruit cups or grapefruit halves for a different taste treat. Add a little syrup to whipped cream as a garnish for waffles, or pour it over sliced bananas and top with whipped cream.

Maple Syrup Popcorn

2 cups sugar
2 cups pure maple syrup
I teaspoon white vinegar
2 tablespoons butter
I cup chopped peanuts
4 quarts popped corn

Combine the sugar, maple syrup, and vinegar and cook over low heat, stirring until the sugar dissolves. Heat to 275°F on a candy thermometer.

Remove from the heat. Add the butter and stir until melted. Add the peanuts, then pour over the popcorn. Blend well.

Yield: 4 quarts

Vermont Maple Syrup Eggnog

2 cups milk
⅓ cup pure maple syrup
3 egg yolks, well beaten
⅛ teaspoon salt
½ cup heavy cream
⅛ teaspoon ginger

Combine the milk, syrup, egg yolks, and salt. Beat until blended and pour into four glasses. Combine the cream and ginger, and top each serving with the mixture.

Serves 4

Down-Home Accompaniments

WHETHER YOU PREFER dining out or eating at home, most repasts center on the entrée. But to me, what turns a merely good dinner into a special one is the accompaniments. Over the years, I have discovered and developed many favorite side dishes that enhance any kind of meal, but that especially lend themselves to fish and game birds.

Many of these recipes indicate that they can be prepared ahead and held overnight or frozen. You can prepare Make-Ahead Mashed Potatoes (page 243) the night before. They serve up creamier and smoother than the just-mashed variety, and are a wonder for the busy cook. And New Orleans Red Beans and Rice (page 242) is downright habit forming.

Nothing included here is ordinary—we all know how to serve buttered carrots and creamed corn. These preparations should stimulate your taste buds and provide an appropriate complement to the entrées that they accompany.

Breads and Pancakes

Branch Road Sourdough Starter

1 package active dry yeast (1 tablespoon)
2½ cups warm water
2 cups flour
1 tablespoon sugar
1 teaspoon salt

Dissolve the yeast in the warm water. Stir in the flour, sugar, and salt and beat until smooth. Let stand, uncovered, at room temperature for 3–5 days. Stir twice daily and cover at night. The mixture will develop a yeasty smell. After 5 days, refrigerate the starter in a crock or glass jar. Bring to room temperature again before using to bake. Every time you remove a portion of starter to bake with, feed the remainder by adding ½ cup warm water, ½ cup flour, and 1 teaspoon sugar to the crock. Stir to blend, and let stand until bubbly and fermented, at least 1 day. Return to the refrigerator, where it will keep indefinitely.

Promised Land Sourdough Cheese and Onion Appetizers

This is an unusual and hearty appetizer, a perfect prelude to a meal of wild game.

1 package active dry yeast (1 tablespoon)

1½ cups warm water

1 cup Branch Road Sourdough Starter (see page 227)

2 teaspoons salt

2 teaspoons sugar

5 to 5½ cups flour

½ teaspoon baking soda

1 medium onion, finely chopped

½ cup grated sharp cheese

½ cup heavy cream

¼ cup cornmeal

Dissolve the yeast in the warm water. Add the starter, salt, sugar, and 2½ cups of the flour. Beat well, cover, and let rise for about 90 minutes, or until doubled. When the dough has risen, preheat the oven to 350°F. Combine the baking soda with 1 cup of the flour and add to the dough, mixing well. Turn out onto a floured surface and knead for 5 minutes, adding the remaining flour as needed to prevent the dough from sticking. Add the onion and knead for 3 minutes. Add the cheese and knead for 3 more minutes. Form the dough into balls the size of walnuts. Dip the top of each ball into the cream and then into the cornmeal. Place the balls about 1 inch apart on a greased baking sheet. Cover with a clean towel and allow to rise in a warm place until doubled in size. Bake until golden brown. Serve warm with cream cheese.

Yield: Approximately 3 dozen appetizers

Grammy Jenet's Rich Scottish Tea Scones

Every time I'm in Great Britain and "take tea," I'm puzzled by my memory of scones compared to everyone else's version of this wonderful treat. Finally I may have found the answer—crumpets. My word, could it be that all that time we were actually making crumpets but calling them scones?

Thanks to my dear friend Ardath and her son William, this recipe seems to be close to what first my Grandma Vance, and then my mother, used to make.

1 tablespoon butter, softened

2 cups flour

2 teaspoons baking powder

¼ cup sugar

1 teaspoon salt

**6 tablespoons very cold butter (¾ stick),
     cut into ¼-inch pieces**

2 eggs

½ cup milk

¼ teaspoon vanilla

Preheat the oven to 400°F. Grease a large baking sheet with the softened butter and set aside. Combine the flour, baking powder, sugar, and salt in a large bowl. Add the 6 tablespoons of cold butter, and rub the flour mixture and butter together with your fingers until flaky. Separate 1 egg, reserving the white, and beat the yolk together with the remaining egg with a whisk until frothy. Beat the milk and vanilla into the egg mixture and pour it over the flour mixture. With your hands or a large spoon, toss the mixture until the dough can be gathered into a ball.

Turn the dough onto a lightly floured surface and dust with flour. Roll out the dough into a ½-inch-thick circle. With a floured cutter or a glass, cut into 2-inch rounds. Place about 1 inch apart on the greased baking sheet. With a fork, beat the reserved egg white briskly and brush it lightly over the tops of the scones. Bake in the middle of the oven for 15–20 minutes, or until golden.

Yield: 12 scones

Crumpets

Now, my mother and grandmother never used flan rings! This is where traditional crumpets seem to part ways with the Vance crumpets that I remember, which are triangles cooked on a griddle. To make the Vance version, I add a bit more flour so the dough will roll out, and cut it into triangles about 3–4 inches long. Then I cook them on the griddle, as below.

1 teaspoon active dry yeast

1 teaspoon sugar

¼ cup warm water

⅓ cup milk

1 egg, slightly beaten

4 tablespoons butter (½ stick), melted

1 cup flour

½ teaspoon salt

4 small flan rings (see *Note*)

Mix the yeast with the sugar and add the water. Let stand for 5 minutes, or until foamy. Stir in the milk, egg, and 2 tablespoons of the butter. Add the flour and salt. Mix well and cover with a damp cloth. Let rise in a warm place until doubled, about 45 minutes. Brush the inside of four flan rings and a griddle with the remaining 2 tablespoons melted butter. Set the flan rings on the griddle and pour or push the batter into the rings. Cook for 7 minutes, or until bubbles form on the top, as on pancakes. Flip and continue to cook until the second side is toasty and the crumpets are cooked through.

Note: Flan rings are bottomless metal rings with straight (about 1½-inch high) metal sides. They can be found in most cookware stores. If you can't find them, substitute tunafish cans, tops and bottoms removed and well washed.

Yield: 4 crumpets, each about the size of an English muffin

Great Smokies Cornbread Cakes

**1¾ cups coarsely ground cornmeal
(preferably stone ground)**

1 cup water

1½ cups buttermilk

2 eggs, beaten

½ cup flour

1 tablespoon salt

1 teaspoon baking powder

¼ teaspoon baking soda

4 tablespoons butter (½ stick), melted

Combine the cornmeal and water, then stir in the buttermilk and beaten eggs. Sift together the flour, salt, baking powder, and baking soda and add to the cornmeal mixture. Blend well to make a thin batter. Drop the batter by spoonfuls onto a hot, lightly greased griddle to make small cakes. Turn once.

Yield: About 12 cakes

Rye Crackers

Make your own crackers? Why not? I love to try the unusual. And I'm so proud to serve homemade crackers with Nig Raney's Jalapeño Pimiento Cheese (see page 239).

1 ⅓ **cups flour**
⅔ **cup rye flour**
½ **teaspoon baking soda**
⅓ **cup vegetable oil**
¼ **cup water**
½ **teaspoon cider vinegar**
¼ **cup caraway seeds**

Preheat the oven to 375°F. Combine the flours and baking soda in a bowl. Add the oil, water, vinegar, and caraway seeds. Stir well, until the mixture forms a ball. On a lightly floured board, roll out the dough ¹⁄₁₆ inch thick. Cut into desired shapes and place on an ungreased cookie sheet. Bake for 12–15 minutes, or until lightly browned. Remove the crackers with a spatula and cool on a wire rack. The crackers may be stored in a tightly covered container for up to 1 week.

Yield: About 3 dozen crackers

Aunt Ruth's Perfect Pear Pecan Bread

This is perhaps the most delicious quick bread ever, and a favorite of my sister-in-law. It's terrific topped with whipped cream cheese, and it freezes well.

½ **cup dark brown sugar**

½ **cup sugar**

½ **cup vegetable oil**

2 **eggs**

¼ **cup sour cream**

1 **teaspoon vanilla extract**

2 **cups flour**

1 **teaspoon baking soda**

½ **teaspoon salt**

½ **teaspoon cinnamon**

¼ **teaspoon freshly grated nutmeg**

1½ **cups coarsely chopped, unpeeled, very ripe pears**

⅔ **cup coarsely chopped pecans**

½ **teaspoon finely grated lemon zest**

Preheat oven to 350°F. Grease a 9 x 5-inch loaf pan. Combine the sugars and the oil and beat well. Add the eggs one at a time, beating well after each addition. Mix in the sour cream and vanilla. Sift together the flour, baking soda, salt, cinnamon, and nutmeg; stir into the batter. Stir in the pears, pecans, and lemon zest. Spoon the batter into the prepared pan. Bake about 1 hour, or until a tester comes out clean. Cool in the pan for 10 minutes, then turn out onto a wire rack to cool completely before slicing.

Note: For a tasty variation, top the batter with toasted sesame seeds before baking.

Yield: 1 loaf

Cranberry Bread

This is an excellent recipe for Thanksgiving dinner. To make delicious party sandwiches, spread thin slices with softened cream cheese and slice into fingers.

2 cups flour
1 cup sugar
1½ teaspoons baking powder
1 teaspoon salt
½ teaspoon baking soda
4 tablespoons butter or margarine (½ stick), softened
¾ cup orange juice
1 tablespoon grated orange zest
1 egg, well beaten
2 cups chopped fresh cranberries
½ cup chopped pecans or walnuts

Preheat the oven to 350°F. Grease a 9 x 5-inch loaf pan. Sift together the flour, sugar, baking powder, salt, and baking soda. Cut in the butter with a pastry blender or a fork until the mixture looks crumbly. Combine the orange juice, orange zest, and egg, and add all at once to the dry ingredients, mixing just enough to moisten. Fold in the cranberries and nuts, mixing just until combined. Pour into the prepared loaf pan and bake for 1 hour, or until the crust is golden brown and a cake tester comes out clean. Cool in the pan for 10 minutes, then turn out onto a wire rack to cool completely. Chill overnight in the refrigerator for easier slicing.

Note: Make Blueberry Bread by substituting blueberries for the cranberries and adding ½ cup of grated cheddar cheese in place of the nuts.

Yield: 1 loaf

Special Pumpkin Bread

3 cups sugar

1 cup vegetable oil

4 eggs, beaten

2 cups cooked pumpkin

3½ cups flour

2 teaspoons baking soda

2 teaspoons salt

1 teaspoon baking powder

1 teaspoon nutmeg

1 teaspoon allspice

1 teaspoon cinnamon

½ teaspoon cloves

⅔ cup water

1 cup chopped walnuts

Grease and flour two 9 x 5-inch loaf pans. Preheat the oven to 350°F. Cream together the sugar and oil until smooth. Add the eggs and pumpkin and mix well. Sift together the flour, baking soda, salt, baking powder, nutmeg, allspice, cinnamon, and cloves. Add the dry ingredients to the pumpkin mixture alternately with the water, mixing well to combine. Add the walnuts and stir thoroughly. Pour into the prepared loaf pans. Bake for 90 minutes, or until a tester comes out clean. Let cool for 10 minutes before removing from the pans.

Note: This bread is also delicious made with ½ cup of raisins and ½ cup of chopped dates. Make party sandwiches by slicing thin, spreading with cream cheese, and cutting into fingers.

Yield: 2 loaves

Perry Road Pancakes and Maple Syrup

1 ¼ cups sifted flour
1 tablespoon baking powder
1 tablespoon sugar
½ teaspoon salt
1 egg, beaten
1 cup buttermilk
2 tablespoons vegetable oil
Buttery Syrup (see below)

Sift together the flour, baking powder, sugar, and salt. In another bowl combine the egg, buttermilk, and oil. Add to the dry ingredients, and stir just until mixed. Cook on a hot, greased griddle. Top with Buttery Syrup.

Yield: about 8 large pancakes

Buttery Syrup

I serve this hot buttered sauce in an old cut-glass pitcher. It looks so much nicer than the syrup bottle on the breakfast table! When you serve it hot, you'll find it doesn't cool down the pancakes and adds buttery goodness.

4 tablespoons butter (½ stick)
1 cup pure maple syrup

Melt the butter in a heavy saucepan. Add the syrup and blend. Heat through, stirring constantly. Serve the hot syrup mixture over pancakes.

Yield: 1¼ cups

Down-Home Accompaniments

Benton Sourdough Buckwheat Cakes

When I was a little girl and waiting to move into our new house, my family lived in the Benton Hotel for several weeks. That grand hotel is gone now, but it was the most imposing structure in Benton, the quiet village in the endless mountains of Columbia County, Pennsylvania, where I grew up. At that time the country was strange enough to me, but stranger still was the yeasty, pungent aroma that filled the dining room and kitchen each evening. It was the smell of buckwheat cakes that permeated that old hotel, and I soon came to love them. They are different, strong-tasting, and very satisfying. They are still featured in several restaurants here, where they are served all day.

Use Branch Road Sourdough Starter to give these buckwheat cakes a savory kick. You'll have to plan about a week ahead, but it's worth the effort!

1 cup lukewarm water

½ cup stirred buckwheat flour

½ cup sifted white flour

1 cup Branch Road Sourdough Starter (page 227)

2 tablespoons brown sugar

2 teaspoons pure maple syrup

½ teaspoon baking soda

½ teaspoon salt

1 tablespoon vegetable oil

Combine the water, buckwheat flour, and white flour with the sourdough starter. Stir until smooth, then let stand overnight. When ready to cook, add the brown sugar, maple syrup, baking soda, and salt. Stir to blend, then add the oil. The batter is now ready for the griddle.

Serves 4–6

O'Douchain's Montana French Toast

*This is a breakfast befitting Montana's Big Sky country—
and the O'Douchain Country Inn in Bigfork does everything
Montana-style.*

1 loaf French bread
2 ripe peaches
½ cup sugar
½ teaspoon cinnamon
6 eggs
¼ cup heavy cream
6 tablespoons butter (¾ stick)
½ cup pure maple syrup

Slice the bread into 3-inch-thick slices. Slit each slice through the middle to form a pocket. (Do not cut the sides and bottom of the bread.) Peel and chop the peaches. Combine the sugar and cinnamon. Toss the peaches in the spiced sugar and spoon into the bread pockets. Press the edges of the bread slices back together.

Beat the eggs and add the cream. Dip the stuffed bread slices in the egg mixture. Melt 4 tablespoons of the butter in a large skillet. Fry the bread until toasted on both sides, turning carefully to retain the peach stuffing. Melt the remaining 2 tablespoons of butter in a small saucepan. Add the syrup and heat through, stirring to combine. Serve hot at the table to pour over the French toast.

Note: I also liked the O'Douchain Country Inn's apple version of this recipe. Substitute grated apples for the peaches—and the result is equally delicious.

Serves 4

Side Dishes

Nig Raney's Jalapeño Pimiento Cheese

I pound rat cheese, grated (Edam or mild cheddar may be substituted)

I small jar chopped pimientos, drained

2 tablespoons Dijon mustard

¼ cup mayonnaise

5 jalapeño peppers, finely chopped

Salt and pepper, to taste

Combine all the ingredients and season to taste with salt and pepper. Add more mayonnaise if necessary to achieve dip consistency. Serve with Rye Crackers (see page 232).

Serves 10–12

Aunt Mag Ginthner's Homemade Noodles

4 eggs
2 cups flour
I teaspoon salt
I to 2 tablespoons cold water

Beat the eggs until lightened. Add the flour and salt and stir to combine; the dough will be very stiff and sticky. Add 1 tablespoon of water and mix until the dough forms a ball, adding another tablespoon of water if necessary. Turn out onto a floured surface, and roll out until the dough is very thin. Allow to rest for 1 hour. Roll up the dough like a jelly roll, and slice across the roll into thin noodles. You can also form dough for potpie noodles. Roll thinly as above, and cut into 1-inch squares. Use in any potpie recipe.

Noodle Variations

1. *Buttered Noodles*. Boil the noodles until tender, about 10–15 minutes, depending on the thickness of the dough. Drain and rinse. Toss with melted butter.
2. *Pennsylvania Dutch Buttered Noodles*. Boil for 10–15 minutes, drain, and rinse. Sauté bread cubes in butter until crisp. Toss the noodles with melted butter and top with the croutons.
3. *Noodles Romanoff*. Boil for 10–15 minutes, drain, and rinse. Toss with 1 pint sour cream, 1 tablespoon Worcestershire sauce, and 1 clove crushed garlic. Top with 1 to 2 tablespoons cracker meal, and bake at 350°F until heated through. This can be made ahead and frozen.

Romanian Noodles

This becomes a truly stellar dish when made with homemade noodles. It is always part of our Christmas buffet table.

Aunt Mag Ginthner's Homemade Noodles (see page 240)
2 cups creamed cottage cheese
1 cup sour cream
1 small onion, minced
¼ teaspoon black pepper
1 teaspoon Worcestershire sauce
2 cloves garlic, grated fine

Preheat the oven to 375°F. Cook the noodles in salted water until tender. Drain and rinse. Mix together the cottage cheese, sour cream, onions, and pepper. When combined, add the Worcestershire sauce and garlic. Fold in the noodles. Pour into a greased casserole and cover with aluminum foil. Cut slits in the foil to let steam escape. Bake for 45 minutes; then remove the foil and bake for 15 minutes more to brown the top.

Note: If you're short on time, you can substitute packaged egg noodles.

Serves 4–6

New Orleans Red Beans and Rice

You know it's good when your son requests red beans and rice for Sunday suppers! And I always include this dish on a buffet table. It's typical Louisiana fare—the South's answer to Italian pasta, and just as good. This is one of my all-time favorites. Plan ahead because the beans must be soaked overnight and the ham hocks simmered for 4–5 hours.

1 pound dried red kidney beans (2 cups)

2 ham hocks

½ pound hot Italian venison sausage (see page 44)

3 cloves garlic, minced

1 teaspoon chili powder or Creole Seasoning (available in cooking shops)

Salt and pepper, to taste

1 cup long-grain white rice

Wash and pick over the beans. Soak overnight in 1 quart of water. Drain, add another 1½ quarts of water to the beans, and place in a slow cooker. Trim all fat and skin off the ham hocks. Add the whole ham hocks to the beans and simmer for 4–5 hours, or until the meat is falling from the bone and the beans are tender. Remove the hocks from the pot and allow to cool.

Cut the sausage into small pieces and add to the beans. Add the garlic, chili powder or Creole seasoning, and salt and pepper, and simmer for another hour. In the meantime, cook the rice according to package directions. Remove the meat from the ham hocks and add to the pot. Cook until the beans can be mashed into the stew, and the stew is very thick. Serve over the hot rice.

Note: Use canned kidney beans to "cheat." While living in Guatemala, I made this with black beans.

Serves 6

Make-Ahead Mashed Potatoes

These mashed potatoes are just as good the next day. For big holiday meals, I make them the night before, eliminating all the mess at the last minute. In fact, when they invite me to a holiday meal, my friends Alice and Kevin usually request that I bring these.

6 to 8 large potatoes
1 (8-ounce) package cream cheese
4 tablespoons butter (½ stick)
Salt, to taste

Peel and quarter the potatoes. Place in a large pot, cover with cold water, and bring to a boil. Boil until tender; drain. Immediately add the cream cheese and butter. Allow to stand until the cheese melts, about 10 minutes. Beat with an electric mixer until smooth. Cover with plastic wrap and refrigerate until ready to serve. Reheat over low heat on the stovetop, stirring often. Add salt to taste.

Note: This can also be reheated in the oven—but who has room in there at holiday time? Microwave on medium heat for 2-minute intervals, stirring in between, until heated through.

Serves 6

Creamed Onions

If you have the patience to deal with the little onions, this dish is well worth the effort. Mother would always "do" the onions at my house. If you want creamy onions and are short of time, try Joyce's Golden Baked Onions (see page 250). They are equally delicious, and a lot easier to prepare.

4 cups small onions
6 tablespoons butter (¾ stick)
2 tablespoons cornstarch
White pepper, to taste
2 cups light cream
½ cup grated Gruyère cheese
Salt, to taste

Score the ends of the onions with a sharp knife. Boil in salted water until fork-tender. Drain and cool. Peel off the skins when cool. Melt the butter in a saucepan over low heat. Blend in the cornstarch and pepper to taste. Add the cream all at once, stirring constantly until the mixture thickens. Remove from the heat as soon as it bubbles. Add the onions and heat through, stirring constantly. Add the cheese and stir to melt, add salt to taste, and serve immediately.

Note: You can prepare these onions ahead and reheat them before serving. Bake at 350°F for 20–25 minutes, until the sauce is bubbly and the onions are heated through.

Serves 6

Thanksgiving Succotash

My mother's dear friend Helen Harvey elevates this simple dish by using her own home-frozen corn.

4 cups fresh or frozen corn
2 cups fresh or frozen lima beans
4 tablespoons butter (½ stick)
½ cup cream
Salt and pepper, to taste

Preheat the oven to 350°F. Boil the corn until tender; drain. Boil the limas until tender; drain. Mix the corn and lima beans together in a baking dish. In a small saucepan, melt the butter and stir in the cream, salt, and pepper. Pour over the vegetables and mix thoroughly. Bake for 20–25 minutes, or until heated through and bubbling.

Serves 6

Potatoes Cooked in Milk

These potatoes are creamy and different. The sharp Italian flavor of fontina cheese adds just enough zing to make them a sure hit.

4 to 6 medium potatoes, peeled and diced
I medium onion, chopped
2 cups milk (or more) to cover potatoes
½ cup grated fontina cheese
Paprika, for garnish

In a heavy saucepan, cover the potatoes and onions with the milk. Simmer slowly, stirring occasionally, for 30–45 minutes, or until fork-tender. When done, remove from the heat and stir in the cheese. Garnish with paprika.

Serves 6

Corn Casserole

What shall we have for a vegetable tonight? Corn, peas, corn, beans, corn . . . This makes a familiar vegetable just a little unusual, and very tasty.

1 tablespoon butter

1 red bell pepper, seeded and chopped

1 cup cracker crumbs

1½ cups evaporated milk

2 eggs, separated

1½ cups fresh or frozen white corn

Pepper, to taste

6 thin slices bacon

Preheat the oven to 350°F. Melt the butter in a skillet and sauté the red peppers. Mix the cracker crumbs, evaporated milk, and well-beaten egg yolks. Beat the egg whites until stiff. Add the corn and red peppers to the liquid mixture and fold in the egg whites. Season with pepper. Pour into a greased baking dish. Arrange the slices of bacon on top and bake for 45 minutes.

Serves 4

Cheesy Rice with Wine

3 tablespoons butter
2 tablespoons sliced green onions
½ cup chopped green bell peppers
1 cup white rice
1 cup chicken stock
½ cup hot water
½ cup dry white wine
¼ cup finely chopped fresh parsley
½ cup grated fontina (or other sharp Italian cheese)

Melt the butter in a heavy saucepan and sauté the onions and peppers until soft. Add the rice and sauté over medium heat, stirring constantly, for 2–3 minutes. Add the stock, water, and wine. Cover tightly. Simmer over low heat for 20–25 minutes, or until the rice is tender but firm. Remove from the heat, toss with the parsley, and turn into an ovenproof serving dish. Top with the cheese and run under the broiler until the cheese is melted.

Note: Sharp cheddar may be substituted for the fontina cheese.

Serves 4

Marinated Carrots

I like veggie recipes that can be prepared ahead of time. When entertaining, I try to do as much as possible the day before so I can "come to my own party."

5 cups carrots, peeled, chopped,   *Marinating time: overnight*
   and cooked until tender
I medium onion, sliced thin
3 medium green onions, including tops, sliced thin
I (8-ounce) can tomato sauce
½ cup water
3 tablespoons tomato paste
½ cup light oil
I teaspoon salt
I teaspoon pepper
I cup sugar
¾ cup white vinegar
I teaspoon Dijon mustard
I teaspoon Worcestershire sauce

Place the cooked carrots in a serving bowl and top with the onions and green onions. Mix the tomato sauce, water, tomato paste, oil, salt, pepper, sugar, vinegar, mustard, and Worcestershire sauce in a blender. Pour over the carrots and onions, cover, and refrigerate overnight to let the flavors blend.

Serves 8

Karen's Broccoli Supreme

My vegetable lovers rate this one a "10," and any cook will love the easy, advance preparation.

2 (10-ounce) packages frozen chopped broccoli
2 (10-ounce) packages frozen chopped spinach
2 cups sour cream
1 package dried onion soup mix
½ cup grated cheddar cheese
¼ cup crumbled blue cheese
½ cup grated Romano cheese

Thaw the broccoli and spinach in a large colander. Preheat the oven to 350°F. Mix the thawed vegetables together with the sour cream, onion soup mix, cheddar cheese, and blue cheese. Pour into a 4-quart baking dish. Top with the grated Romano. Bake for 45 minutes, or until the edges bubble and the cheese turns golden.

Note: This is better if mixed a day in advance and refrigerated overnight.

Serves 6–8

Joyce's Golden Baked Onions

Just as good as Creamed Onions (see page 244), but much easier. My friend Alice requests this dish often, and I never visit her without a casserole of baked onions in my arms.

8 tablespoons butter (1 stick)
6 medium onions, sliced
1 (10-ounce) can cream of chicken soup
1 cup evaporated milk
¼ teaspoon salt
¼ teaspoon cayenne pepper
1 cup Swiss cheese, grated
½ loaf French bread, sliced

Preheat the oven to 350°F. Grease a 2-quart baking dish. Melt the butter in a large skillet over medium heat; add the onions and cook until they are tender and translucent, stirring frequently. With a slotted spoon, transfer the onions to the baking dish, reserving the butter in the skillet. In a bowl, combine the soup, evaporated milk, salt, and cayenne and pour over the onions. Sprinkle with the grated cheese.

Dip the bread slices in the reserved melted butter on one side. Arrange the bread slices, buttered-side up, over the onion mixture to cover completely. Bake about 30 minutes, until the bread is browned and the onions bubbly.

Serves 4

Coopersburg Corn Chowder

This is a very rich and satisfying soup, a meal in itself.

2 tablespoons butter or margarine
1 medium onion, chopped
1 cup chopped celery
1 (16-ounce) can creamed corn
4 cups milk
2 cups grated sharp cheese
1 tablespoon Old Bay Seafood Seasoning
1 teaspoon oregano
1 teaspoon basil
1 teaspoon paprika

In a soup pot, melt the butter (or margarine) and sauté the onions and celery. Add the corn, milk, cheese, and seasonings, and bring to a boil. Reduce the heat immediately and simmer for 15–20 minutes, to allow the flavors to blend.

Serves 6

Salads

Make-Ahead Vegetable Salad

Do anything you can the day before a big meal or a party. I love "do-ahead" recipes.

2 cups raw cauliflower   *Marinating time: overnight*
1 pound green beans, blanched,
    trimmed, and chopped
¼ pound mushrooms, sliced
1 cup olives, pitted and sliced
1 onion, sliced
½ cup lemon juice
½ cup vegetable oil
2 tablespoons sugar
1 teaspoon dill
2 cups shredded iceberg lettuce

Layer the cauliflower, beans, mushrooms, and olives in a large glass bowl and top with the onion slices. Combine the lemon juice, oil, sugar, and dill. Pour over the vegetables, cover, and refrigerate overnight. Top with the shredded lettuce just before serving.

Serves 6

Sally Keehn's Spinach Salad

Sally and I were in the Bucks County Writers Group, headed by the late Helen Papashvily. Helen's charm, charisma, and talent helped us navigate the choppy waters of the literary world. We all loved her and miss her terribly.

Dressing
½ **cup sugar**
¼ **cup white vinegar**
¼ **cup light corn oil**
¼ **cup water**
3 **teaspoons Dijon mustard**
½ **teaspoon pepper**
1 **medium onion, chopped**

10 **ounces fresh spinach**
½ **pound bacon, fried crisp**
2 **cups croutons**
3 **hard-cooked eggs**

For the dressing, combine the sugar, vinegar, oil, water, mustard, pepper, and onions, and blend well.

Wash, dry, and stem the spinach and tear into bite-sized pieces. Place in a large salad bowl and pour the dressing over it. Add the bacon and croutons and toss to mix. Garnish with grated or sliced hard-cooked eggs.

Note: Make the dressing for this salad a day ahead, if possible, and refrigerate it overnight to allow the flavors to blend more completely.

Serves 4

Rice Salad

This is a good, quick cold salad that takes half the time of potato salad.

2 cups cooked white rice
I cup chopped celery
I medium onion, chopped
½ cup sliced green onions, including tops
I cup pimiento-stuffed green olives, sliced
I cup sour cream
I cup mayonnaise

Combine all ingredients and chill several hours or overnight.

Note: Use no-fat sour cream and reduced-fat mayonnaise for fewer calories and less fat.

Serves 6–8

Green Bean Salad

This is a great alternative to a lettuce salad. Just don't overcook the beans.

I pound fresh green beans   *Marinating time: 1–2 hours*
½ large sweet onion, sliced very thin
½ cup vegetable oil
¼ cup vinegar
I clove garlic, crushed
½ teaspoon oregano
Dash pepper
Pinch sugar

Cook the beans until crisp-tender, then drain. Place in a serving dish and cover with the onion slices. Combine the oil, vinegar, garlic, oregano, pepper, and sugar and pour over the vegetables. Refrigerate for 1–2 hours to allow the flavors to blend. Toss just before serving.

Serves 4

Karen's Favorite Potato Salad

½ cup salad oil

¼ cup vinegar

1 tablespoon salt

¼ teaspoon pepper

8 cups hot diced, cooked potatoes

¾ cup chopped green olives

2 or 3 dill pickles, chopped

4 hard-cooked eggs, diced

2 cups diced celery

1 onion, chopped

1 cup salad dressing or mayonnaise

Mix together the oil, vinegar, salt, and pepper. Pour over the hot potatoes. Cool. Mix in the olives, pickles, hard-cooked eggs, celery, onions, and salad dressing. Chill.

Serves 6

My Niece Misho's Layered Salad

I love being able to do as much ahead of time as possible, and here at last is a salad that will actually keep overnight. Assemble this the day before serving and you'll be amazed at how delicious and fresh it will be. Vary the vegetables to your taste. If you don't choose to make it the day before, be sure to assemble the salad at least 2 hours before the meal. A deep glass bowl shows this salad off beautifully.

½ **medium head of lettuce, shredded**

2 **cups ripe cherry tomatoes, halved**

1 **cup ripe olives (optional)**

2 **cups fresh peas, cooked**

½ **cup chopped ham**

½ **cup julienned green bell peppers**

½ **cup diced celery**

1 **medium mild onion, thinly sliced and separated into rings**

1 **cup or more mayonnaise**

1 **cup grated sharp cheddar cheese**

½ **pound bacon, fried crisp and crumbled, for garnish**

Marinating time: 2 hours, or overnight

Layer all the ingredients except the mayonnaise, cheese, and bacon, in a deep glass bowl, starting and ending with the lettuce. Spread the top of the salad with the mayonnaise; depending on the circumference of your bowl, you may need more than 1 cup. The mayonnaise layer should be about ¾ inch thick, and should extend to the sides of the bowl to seal the salad. Top with the grated cheese and refrigerate until serving time. Garnish with the bacon and serve immediately. Toss this salad at the table.

Serves 6

Cranberry Salad

This is a delicious, beautiful salad or side dish. It's very effective with ham or fowl.

I navel orange
½ cup canned crushed pineapple
I (3-ounce) package cherry gelatin dessert
I (16-ounce) can whole berry cranberry sauce
I rib celery, finely chopped
I apple, finely chopped
¼ cup chopped walnuts

Peel the orange, cut it into sections, and pulse in a blender until it is reduced to fine pieces. Drain the pineapple and reserve the juice. Measure the juice and add enough boiling water to make 1 cup of liquid. In a medium bowl, mix the gelatin with 1 cup of boiling water. Stir well, and add the pineapple juice. Stir in the cranberry sauce, then chill. When the mixture is thick, add the celery, apples, walnuts, and orange puree. Pour into a 9 x 13-inch pan and chill. After 30 minutes, stir to redistribute the ingredients, and return to the refrigerator. Serve when firm.

Serves 6

Strawberry Mold

2 (3-ounce) packages strawberry gelatin dessert
1 (8-ounce) can crushed pineapple
1 (12-ounce) package frozen strawberries, thawed
3 medium bananas, mashed
½ pint sour cream
½ cup finely crushed pecans

Dissolve the gelatin in 1½ cups of boiling water. Add the pineapple with its juice. Then add the strawberries with their juice, and the mashed bananas. Pour half the mixture into a 2-quart gelatin mold and chill in the refrigerator until firm. Keep the other half of the mixture at room temperature. Spread the sour cream over the chilled half, sprinkle with the pecans, then pour the room-temperature gelatin mixture over the sour cream. Refrigerate until set. Unmold to serve.

Serves 8

Desserts

THE VANCES ARE NOT big dessert eaters. For any of us to succumb, the offering must be extra special and very tempting. There are not many preparations in this section for that reason—it's difficult to qualify for inclusion here. While some of these recipes may sound familiar, they are all just a little richer, creamier, and more flavorful than other desserts.

Bananas Foster

This recipe is from the New Orleans School of Cooking, and this scrumptious dessert always reminds me of my many visits to that flamboyant city.

2 bananas, sliced in half lengthwise
4 tablespoons butter (½ stick), melted
1 cup dark brown sugar
½ cup rum
¼ cup banana liqueur
½ teaspoon cinnamon

Place the bananas cut-side down in a baking dish. Cream together the melted butter and brown sugar to form a paste. Add the banana liqueur, rum, and cinnamon. Pour the rum mixture over the bananas. For a spectacular effect, ignite the rum at the table .

Serves 4

Deluxe, Very Wicked Chocolate Rum Pie

This is a very, very rich pie; serve in small pieces. If made in the blender, the filling has the consistency of a smooth chocolate bar. Food processors and mixers do not produce the same consistency.

12 tablespoons butter (1½ sticks), softened
1 cup sugar
Frozen egg substitute equivalent to 5 eggs (see Note)
3 (1-ounce) squares unsweetened baking chocolate, melted
⅓ cup dark rum
1 (9-inch) pie shell, baked and cooled (see page 263)
1 cup cream, whipped
Chocolate curls for garnish (optional)

Cream the butter and sugar in a blender; do not use a mixer or food processor. Add the egg substitute and the melted chocolate and blend until dark and smooth. Pour in the rum and blend for several more seconds. Pour into the prepared pie shell, and then refrigerate for at least 3 hours. Garnish with the whipped cream and chocolate curls, if desired.

Note: I call for frozen egg substitute instead of whole raw eggs in this recipe to avoid the risk of salmonella.

Yield: 1 (9-inch) pie

Pear Perfection

This is a very elegant dessert and a perfect way to conclude a fish or seafood meal.

8 ripe pears
1 cup rosé wine
½ cup sugar
⅓ cup red currant jelly
½ cup orange juice
½ teaspoon vanilla extract
2 whole cloves
1 stick cinnamon
Whipped cream, for garnish (optional)

Carefully pare the skin from the whole pears, leaving the stems attached. In a saucepan, combine the wine, sugar, and jelly over medium heat. Stir frequently until the jelly melts. Add the orange juice, vanilla, cloves, and cinnamon stick. Add the pears and simmer for 40–45 minutes, or until the pears are transparent at the edges. Remove the pears to a deep bowl. Boil the syrup until very thick, 20–25 minutes, stirring frequently. Pour the syrup over the pears and chill for several hours or overnight. Serve individual pears in tall-stemmed goblets and top with whipped cream.

Note: The longer the pears marinate in the sauce, the more flavorful they become. To hold them overnight, store in a plastic bag to prevent them from drying out or discoloring. Make sure each pear is covered with sauce and press out any excess air before sealing the bag.

Serves 8

Baked Peaches

This is a nice change of pace during peach season. It's very pretty served in glass bowls, with the red sauce from the baking dish poured over for color.

6 large peaches

2 tablespoons butter

1½ tablespoons sugar

¾ cup vanilla wafer crumbs

¼ cup shredded fresh coconut

1 egg, beaten

1 tablespoon Cognac

4 tablespoons sweet vermouth

¼ cup water

Preheat the oven to 350°F. Cut the peaches in half, remove the pits, and peel. Scoop out a little of the pulp to accommodate the stuffing. Cream together the butter and sugar. Mash the scooped-out peach pulp and add to the creamed mixture. Mix together the vanilla wafer crumbs, coconut, egg, and Cognac. Add to the batter, stirring well to combine. Stuff the peach halves with the filling and arrange them in a buttered baking dish. Sprinkle 1 teaspoon of the vermouth on each stuffed peach half. Pour the water into the dish. Bake for 25 minutes, or until peaches are tender but still firm.

Serves 6

Miracle Piecrust

*Before this recipe, pie making was enough to send me to the edge
of despair. My pie plates were filled with irregular, puzzlelike
pieces of dough rudely pressed together in the hopes that the
miracle of baking would render them whole. It rarely did. You can
throw this miracle dough over your head before placing it in the
pie pan, and it will still make a perfect crust.*

4 cups flour
1 ½ cups vegetable shortening (see *Note*)
1 teaspoon salt
1 teaspoon sugar
1 egg
½ cup cold water
1 teaspoon vinegar

Using a pastry blender, combine the flour, shortening, salt, and sugar to
make particles the size of peas. Beat the egg and add the water and vinegar. Add the egg mixture to the flour mixture and blend until just mixed
through. Divide the dough into five equal parts and roll each part on a
floured board to the desired thickness.

Note: Lard is the shortening traditionally used by the Pennsylvania
Dutch grammy who gave me this recipe. It yields manageable, yet rich
and flaky, crusts every time.

Yield: 5 pie shells, or enough for 3 two-crust pies

Pumpkin Pecan Pie

I seem to have a talent for taking something that is already fatten-ing and making it over-the-top! This is an over-the-top pie. Make it once a year, and don't worry about the calories!

3 eggs, slightly beaten
I cup cooked pumpkin
I cup light brown sugar
½ cup corn syrup
I teaspoon vanilla extract
½ teaspoon cinnamon
¼ teaspoon ginger
¼ teaspoon salt
I unbaked 9-inch pie shell (see page 263)
I cup chopped pecans
Whipped cream

Preheat the oven to 350°F. In a small mixing bowl, mix the eggs, pump-kin, sugar, corn syrup, vanilla, cinnamon, ginger, and salt. Pour into the unbaked pastry shell and sprinkle the pecans on top. Bake for 40 min-utes. Chill. Serve with whipped cream.

Yield: 1 (9-inch) pie

Grandma Betty Ruckle's Lemon Sponge Pie

Grandma Betty, as my grandsons call her, is famous locally for this pie, and it is usually her contribution to family dinners. She often prepares the lemon juice and zest in advance, then freezes them in individual pie portions. She also keeps homemade pie shells in the freezer, so you can see how easy it would be to whip up one of these pies on short notice. The official family historian, Betty keeps a daily journal, so we use her to settle such disputes as how much snow fell in 1980, how many ears of corn were frozen in 1991, and what the weather was like when the grandchildren were born.

2 tablespoons butter

1 cup sugar

4 eggs, separated

2 tablespoons flour

1 cup milk

⅓ cup lemon juice

1 teaspoon lemon zest

¼ teaspoon salt

1 unbaked pie shell (see page 263)

Preheat the oven to 375°F. Cream the butter and sugar. Add the egg yolks and beat until blended. Add the flour, milk, lemon juice, and lemon zest. Beat the reserved egg whites with the salt until foamy. Fold into the lemon mixture, then pour into the unbaked pie shell. Bake for 30–35 minutes, or until the pie is set and a knife inserted in the center comes out clean.

Yield: 1 (9-inch) pie

Double Lemon Pie

2 lemons
¼ cup lemon juice
1 ¼ cups plus 3 tablespoons sugar
2 tablespoons flour
4 tablespoons butter (½ stick)
2 eggs
¼ cup water
1 unbaked 9-inch pie shell (see page 263)
½ teaspoon cinnamon
1 egg white, beaten until frothy

Preheat the oven to 400°F. Cut one of the lemons in half; grate and reserve the zest of one lemon half, then squeeze the juice from the half and add it to the ¼ cup lemon juice; you should now have ½ cup. Store the remaining lemon half for another use. Slice the remaining whole lemon very, very thinly. In a small bowl, with an electric mixer at medium speed, beat 1¼ cups of the sugar, the flour, and butter until the mixture is coarsely crumbled. Slowly beat in the eggs, water, reserved lemon zest, and lemon juice. Fold in the lemon slices. Pour into the unbaked pie crust and bake for 20–30 minutes. Remove from the oven. Mix the cinnamon with the remaining 3 tablespoons of sugar. Brush the top of the pie with the beaten egg white and sprinkle with the cinnamon and sugar. Bake for 10 minutes more.

Yield: 1 (9-inch) pie

Mud Pie

1 gallon coffee ice cream
1½ cups chocolate wafer cookie crumbs (about 20 wafers)
4 tablespoons butter (½ stick), melted
1 (12-ounce) jar chocolate fudge sauce
½ cup salted peanuts, chopped
½ pint heavy cream, whipped

Soften the ice cream at room temperature until it is spreadable. Meanwhile, combine the chocolate cookie crumbs and the butter. Press the mixture into the bottom and sides of a 9-inch pie plate, reserving some crumbs for garnish, if desired. Chill. Fill the chilled chocolate crust with the softened ice cream. Top with the fudge sauce and sprinkle the peanuts around the outside of the pie. Freeze for several hours, until firm. Garnish with the whipped cream.

Note: The crumbs for this piecrust are easy to make if you break up the cookies and put them, several at a time, into a blender or food processor. Pulse on and off a few times until you have crumbs.

Yield: 1 (9-inch) pie

Aunt Mary's Ice Cream Pie

When we go to visit Aunt Mary and Uncle Eddie in Maryland, we can be sure we'll be treated to ice cream pie. The trick to making this pie is obeying the directions . . . especially the word "cool." Do not rush and try to finish the pie before the marshmallow mixture is cool. Test on the inside of your wrist, as for a baby bottle, and proceed only when the mixture is tepid. This pie is creamy and smooth and delicious.

1½ cups chocolate wafer crumbs
⅓ cup butter, melted
½ pound marshmallows (30 to 32)
1 cup milk
1 teaspoon vanilla extract
1 cup heavy cream
Shredded coconut or crushed peanuts, for garnish
Maraschino cherry, for garnish (optional)

Combine the crumbs and the butter. Press firmly into a 9-inch pie pan and chill until firm. Meanwhile, heat the marshmallows and the milk together in a double boiler, stirring occasionally, until the marshmallows are melted. Allow to cool thoroughly, then stir in the vanilla. Whip the heavy cream and fold into the marshmallow mixture. Pour into the pie shell. Form a ring of coconut or crushed nuts around the rim of the pie. Place the maraschino cherry in the center, if desired. Freeze, uncovered, until frozen solid. Before serving, allow the pie to sit at room temperature for 15–20 minutes to soften.

Note: To store, wrap the thoroughly frozen pie in plastic wrap, then freezer paper. It will keep in the freezer for 1–2 months.

Yield: 1 (9-inch) pie

Moosehead Lodge Oatmeal Cookies

Mary Taggert and her husband Mal own and operate Moosehead Lodge near Messines, Québec. Mary adds these cookies to the delicious lunches she packs whenever guests embark on a daylong adventure. They were so good that some of us were inventing "trips" in order to get more cookies!

1 pound butter (4 sticks), softened

2 cups white sugar

1 cup brown sugar

2 eggs, beaten

2 teaspoons vanilla extract

2½ cups whole-wheat flour

4 teaspoons baking powder

1½ cups rolled oats

1 cup bran

Preheat the oven to 325°F. Cream the butter with the brown and white sugars. Add the eggs and vanilla. Combine the flour, baking powder, oats, and bran, and add to the sugar-and-egg mixture. Shape into balls or drop by spoonfuls onto an ungreased cookie sheet. Flatten with a fork. Bake for 10–12 minutes. Allow to cool for several minutes before removing from the pan.

Yield: 2 dozen cookies

Orange Nut Cake

This is a delicious, rich, pound-cake-type dessert—excellent served with Irish coffee.

Zest of 1 orange
½ cup chopped pecans
2¾ cups flour
2 cups sugar
2¼ teaspoons baking powder
1 teaspoon salt
½ pound butter (2 sticks)
1 teaspoon orange extract
½ cup Triple Sec
½ cup milk
4 eggs, beaten

Grease and flour a 9-inch tube pan. Preheat the oven to 325°F. Reserve 2 teaspoons of the orange zest for the cake batter. Put the remaining orange zest and pecans in the bottom of the pan. Combine the flour, 1¾ cups of the sugar, baking powder, and salt and add the butter, orange extract, Triple Sec, and milk. Beat for 2 minutes. Add the eggs and the reserved orange zest and beat until smooth. Pour the batter over the nuts and zest already in the pan. Bake for 50–60 minutes. Cool for 20 minutes before turning out of the pan. Sprinkle the remaining ¼ cup of sugar on top while the cake is still warm.

Yield: 1 (9-inch) tube cake

Crazy Chocolate Cake

This is a great cake to make in a hurry. The ingredients are common and always available in everyone's cupboard. In addition to being economical and easy, it is one of the darkest and most moist chocolate cake recipes I've ever come across.

My grandsons, Austin and Ethan, love to make this cake. When they were little, they called it a project. "Let's make a chocolate cake project, Gram!" We ice it with whipped topping and there's never a crumb left.

3 cups flour

2 cups sugar

¾ cup cocoa

1 teaspoon salt

2 teaspoons baking soda

2 cups water

¾ cup vegetable oil

2 tablespoons vinegar

2 teaspoons vanilla extract

Preheat the oven to 350°F. Butter and flour 2 layer cake pans or a 13 x 9-inch pan. Sift together the flour, sugar, cocoa, salt, and baking soda. Mix together the water, oil, vinegar, and vanilla. Pour into the dry ingredients and mix until smooth. Pour into the pan or pans and bake for 40–45 minutes.

Yield: 2 (9-inch) layer cakes or 1 (13 x 9-inch) sheet cake.

Quick and Easy Carrot Cake

I cup white sugar

I cup dark brown sugar

I ½ cups vegetable oil

4 eggs, well beaten

2 cups flour

2 teaspoons baking powder

2 teaspoons baking soda

2 teaspoons cinnamon

I teaspoon salt

2 cups grated carrots

I cup chopped walnuts

I cup canned crushed pineapple, drained

Frosting

3 ounces cream cheese, softened

I tablespoon warm water

I teaspoon vanilla extract

3 cups sifted confectioner's sugar

Preheat the oven to 325°F. Grease and flour a 9 x 13-inch cake pan. Combine the white and brown sugars, oil, and eggs and mix well. Sift together the flour, baking powder, baking soda, cinnamon, and salt. Combine with the sugar mixture and stir until smooth. Stir in the carrots, walnuts, and pineapple. Scrape into the pan and bake for 45 minutes.

While the cake is baking, make the frosting. Beat the cream cheese until smooth, then beat in the water and vanilla. Gradually add the confectioner's sugar, beating until smooth and spreadable. When the cake is done, cool in the pan. Spread the frosting on top of the cake and serve.

Yield: 1 (13 x 9-inch) sheet cake

New Orleans Pralines

Pronounced prawleens, *these delicacies came to us from France, where almonds were used. With pecans so prevalent in the South, the French sweet became Americanized into the tempting pecan treat it is today. This recipe comes from the New Orleans School of Cooking.*

1 ½ **cups white sugar**
¾ **cup light brown sugar, packed**
½ **cup milk**
6 **tablespoons butter (¾ stick)**
1 ½ **cups pecans**

Combine all the ingredients in a saucepan. Stirring constantly, heat the mixture to the soft-ball stage (238–240°F on a candy thermometer). Remove from the heat and stir until the candy cools and thickens. Spoon out onto buttered wax paper, aluminum foil, or parchment paper to harden. Break apart into pieces and store in an airtight container.

Yield: 2–3 dozen pralines

Joe Cahn's Bread Pudding

My Aunt Peg makes this regularly for her neighbor Johnny, who shovels her walk, pulls her weeds, and cuts her lawn. I make it for my annual open house after the Christmas program at church, and it disappears. This is an embellished version of what was my father's favorite dessert. I know he'd love this one.

1 (10-ounce) loaf stale French bread, crumbled
   (or 6 to 8 cups any type bread)

4 cups milk

2 cups sugar

4 tablespoons butter (½ stick), melted

3 eggs, lightly beaten

2 tablespoons vanilla extract

1 cup raisins

1 cup coconut

1 cup chopped pecans

1 teaspoon cinnamon

1 teaspoon nutmeg

Whiskey Sauce (see next page)

Combine all ingredients; the mixture should be very moist but not soupy. Pour into a buttered 9 x 9-inch baking dish. Place into a cold oven, turn the temperature to 350°F, and bake for approximately 1 hour and 15 minutes, or until the top is golden brown. Serve warm with Whiskey Sauce.

Serves 16–20

Whiskey Sauce

8 tablespoons butter (1 stick)
1 ½ cups confectioner's sugar
1 egg yolk
½ cup bourbon (or to taste)

Cream the butter and confectioner's sugar in a saucepan over medium heat until all the butter is absorbed. Remove from the heat and beat in the egg yolk. Pour in the bourbon gradually to your own taste, stirring constantly. The sauce will thicken as it cools. Serve warm over warm bread pudding.

Note: Fruit juice or liqueur can be substituted for the bourbon.

Café Brûlot

An elegant way to end a meal, from the New Orleans School of Cooking.

½ tablespoon butter
5 whole cloves
8 curls orange peel
8 curls lemon peel
4 teaspoons dark brown sugar
½ cup brandy
¼ cup Triple Sec
Ground cinnamon
2 cups strong hot New Orleans coffee (or your favorite blend)

Place the butter, cloves, orange peel, lemon peel, brown sugar, brandy, and Triple Sec in a deep chafing dish or brûlot bowl over a flame. Heat and ignite. Agitate to keep the flame burning, and add a few pinches of ground cinnamon to the flame. Pour the hot coffee into the dish or bowl and let the flames go out. Serve immediately in demitasse cups.

Serves 4

Grandma Magagna's Chocolate Peanut Butter Fudge

This is the most delicious fudge I have ever tasted—anywhere.
Even someone without a sweet tooth cannot leave it alone.

½ **pound butter (2 sticks)**
3 tablespoons cocoa
I cup peanut butter (creamy or crunchy)
I teaspoon vanilla extract
I pound confectioner's sugar (see Note)

Line a jelly roll pan with wax paper. Melt the butter, add the cocoa, and stir until it dissolves. Stir in the peanut butter and vanilla and beat until smooth. Add the confectioner's sugar and mix until smooth. Pour into the lined pan. Cut into squares when cool.

Note: Grandma says, "I have an electric stove. As soon as the butter is melted, I turn my heat off and add the cocoa. Then remove from stove. I use my hands to mix the sugar completely into the batter."

I say, "Don't measure the sugar. Buy a 1-pound bag and use it. I have had this recipe fail because I was using the remains of several bags of confectioner's sugar and tried to measure rather than weigh 1 pound. Because it is so light, go by weight."

Yield: 2 dozen squares

Sources

Broken Arrow Ranch
P.O. Box 530
Ingram, TX 78025
1-800-962-4263
Free-range venison and ante-
lope

GoodHeart Specialty Meats Co.
11122 Nacogdoches Road
San Antonio, TX 78217
1-888-466-3992;
FAX: 210-637-1391
web site: www.goodheart.com

Gourmet Game Meats and
Foodstuffs from L.F.C.
954-964-5861;
FAX: 954-964-6148
e-mail: eatgame@msn.com

MacFarlane Pheasant Farm
2821 U.S. Highway 51
Janesville, WI 53546
608-757-7881; 1-800-345-8348
FAX: 608-757-7884
web site: www.pheasant.com
Game birds and meats

Musicon, Inc.
157 Scotchtown Road
Goshen, NY 10924
Farm-raised venison

Old World Venison Co.
Route 1, Box 262
Randall, MN 56475
320-749-2197
e-mail: pbingham@upstel.net
web site: http//www.upstel.net/
pbingham/venison.html

Venison America
P.O. Box 86
Rosemount, MN 55068
1-800-310-2360
e-mail: info@venisonamerica.
com

Venison World Products
1-800-460-5326
FAX: 915-869-7220
web site:
http//www.venison.com/
products.html

Index